ACUPUNCTURE

HOW IT WORKS, HOW IT CURES

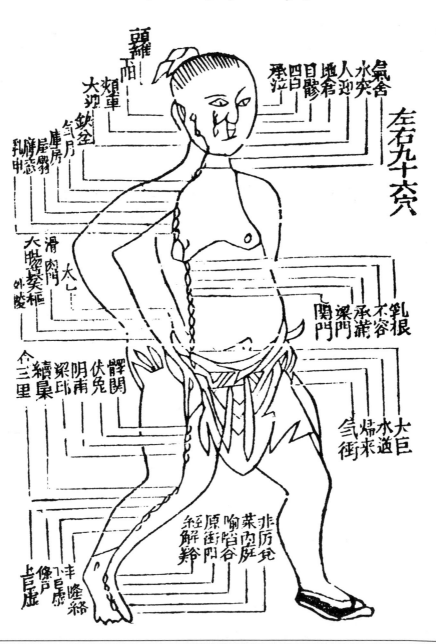

ACUPUNCTURE

HOW IT WORKS, HOW IT CURES

Peter Firebrace

Sandra Hill

Members of the International register of Oriental Medicine

Keats Publishing, Inc.  New Canaan, Connecticut

Dedicated to
Dr J. D. van Buren, Claude Larre s.j., Dr H.
Motoyama and Dr Thomas Maughan for
their pioneering work towards a new
understanding of medicine.

Acupuncture: How It Works, How it Cures is not intended as medical
advice. Its intent is solely informational and educational. Please con-
sult a health professional should the need for one be indicated.

ACUPUNCTURE: HOW IT WORKS, HOW IT CURES
Published by arrangement with Constable & Company, Limited
Copyright © 1994 Peter Firebrace and Sandra Hill
All rights reserved
No part of this book may be reproduced in any form without the writ-
ten consent of the publisher

Library of Congress Cataloging-in-Publication Data

Firebrace, Peter
    Acupuncture: how it works, how it cures / Peter Firebrace, Sandra
Hill.
        p.   cm.
    Originally published in London under title: A guide to acupunc-
ture.
    Includes bibliographical references and index.
    ISBN 0-87983-639-3 : $19.95
    1. Acupuncture--Popular works. I. Hill, Sandra. II Title.
RM184.F559 1993   93-46610
615.8'92--dc20   CIP

Printed by Mandarin Offset in Hong Kong
Published by Keats Publishing, Inc.
27 Pine Street (Box 876)
New Canaan, CT 06840-0876

CONTENTS

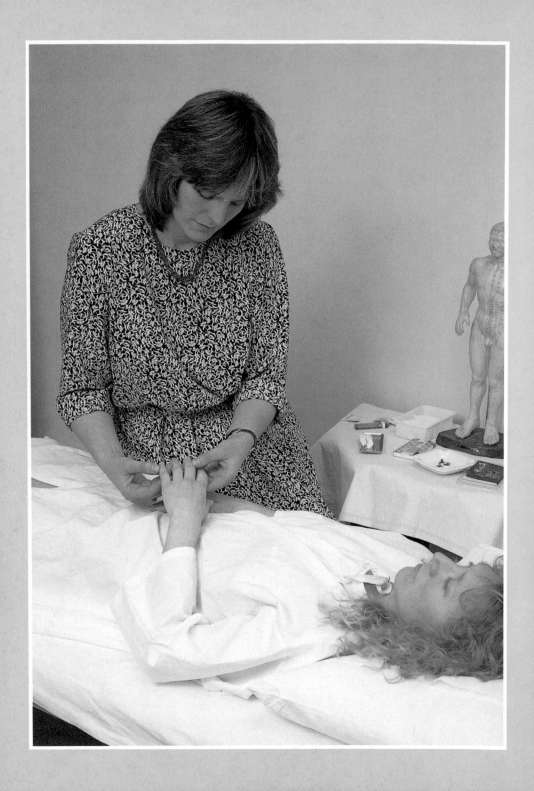

1

INTRODUCTION

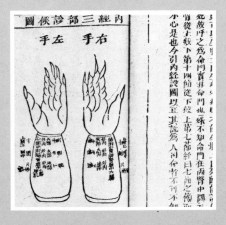

For thousands of years, the Chinese and other Eastern peoples have been using acupuncture to restore, promote and maintain good health. To the Chinese today, it is as much the norm to see an acupuncturist or doctor of traditional Chinese medicine as it is for us to visit our own doctors of Western medicine. They will expect to be asked questions about their health, have their tongue examined, the pulses taken at the wrist and, after due consideration from the doctor, to be treated by the insertion of fine needles at specific points on the body.

For most Westerners considering acupuncture for the first time, however, such an experience raises many questions. What can an acupuncturist determine from an examination of the tongue? What can he tell from the pulse? Why are the needles put in a particular place? What do the needles do? How can it work? Will it hurt?

To go some way towards answering these questions and to clarify the scope and extent of acupuncture is the purpose of this book. This cannot be done easily, however, because acupuncture, its philosophy and its practice is a large and complex subject, which has a 2,000-year written history. Without this unique perspective, acupuncture cannot be understood, and cannot be effectively used for treatment. It is rooted in the *Daoist* philosophy of change and growth, balance and harmony, and some familiarity with these concepts is essential for understanding.

The self-healing body
Central to the concepts behind acupuncture is the idea of the body as self-healing – that as living beings we are all naturally full of vitality and are continually, and quite unconsciously, being rebalanced and regenerated from within. This is not difficult to understand. Cuts heal 'on their own'; women have the creative power to develop and produce children 'on their own', and the children in their turn grow and develop from babies to toddlers, young children to teenagers, teenagers to adults – all 'on their own'.

In a similar way, food is broken down, transformed and separated into useful parts that are absorbed by the body and useless parts that are evacuated – all automatically, without any conscious or outside interference. In other words, there is a great source – and resource – within the body that continually maintains order, working ceaselessly for our benefit and health.

Acupuncture sees the body as a self-rectifying dynamic whole, a network of interrelating and interacting energies. Their even distribution and flow maintains health, but any interruption, depletion or stagnation leads to disease. Acupuncture is a system of medicine which seeks to aid these natural processes, helping the body to correct itself by a realignment or redirection of energy, which the Chinese call *Qi* (pronounced 'chee').

Qi energy

The concept of *Qi* is difficult to define, although everybody really knows what it is. It is often translated as breath, lifeforce, vitality, energy or simply as that which makes us alive. If there is no *Qi,* there is no life. A wilting plant is lacking in *Qi*; a feeble person and a weak voice both show a lack of *Qi*; strong, lively, energetic people have plenty of *Qi*. There is a lot of *Qi* at a children's party; and there is a lot of *Qi* in quiet strength. In illness, the *Qi* is depleted, causing tiredness and depression; or it may be disturbed, causing irritability and over-reaction.

All of us know from our own experience what this *Qi* is and when it is flowing smoothly. Acupuncture makes a detailed study of *Qi*, dividing it into many different kinds depending on its function – such as nourishing or protecting. The proper quality, distibution and even flow of *Qi* is of the utmost importance to health.

The meridian system

Along with the notion of *Qi*, acupuncture recognizes a subtle energy system by which *Qi* is circulated through the body in a network of channels or 'meridians'. Along these meridians or channels lie the acupuncture points, and when an acupuncture needle is inserted it is the *Qi* that is affected. This interlacing network of meridians is the crux of traditional acupuncture.

The Chinese themselves have compared the flow of *Qi* through the meridian system to water irrigating the land: feeding, nourishing and sustaining the substance through which it flows. It is similar in some ways to the blood circulation and nervous system but is invisible to the eye, although it can be sensed from its effects by a trained practitioner and has been charted since more than 2,000 years ago. By needling the points, the *Qi* can be 'tapped' or affected to influence the state of health.

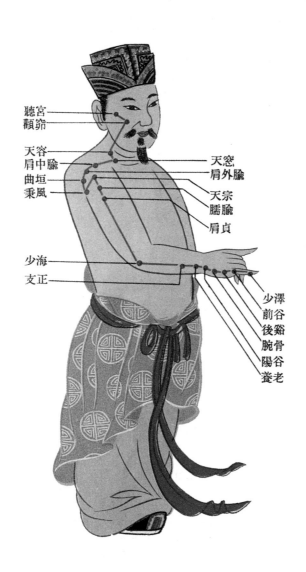

聽宮
顴窌

天容
肩中腧
曲垣
秉風

少海
支正

天窗
肩外腧

天宗
臑腧
肩貞

少澤
前谷
後谿
腕骨
陽谷
養老

手太陽小腸經之圖　凡一十九穴　左右共三十八穴

圖五十六——仿明版古圖(二)

In another analogy the Chinese describe the body as a musical instrument, constantly resounding with the flow of Qi in the meridians, as a flute does with a breath of air. Good health is the equivalent of a pure clear note from this instrument, and illness as discord, which can be corrected by stimulating different points or holes, thus altering the quality of the note. These ideas of tuning (which nowadays we might also think of in relation to the engine of a car) and allied ideas of correct frequency, timing, and so on to ensure that things run well, are useful analogies for us in the modern world. Interestingly it is not regarded as entirely coincidental that many of the theoretical principles of modern physics have a similar basis and 'world view' as acupuncture. Both are looking behind the scenes at the interaction of energies. Acupuncture may be old – but its principles are also very modern!

The holistic approach to disease

From an understanding of the body as an energetic and vibrating whole comes a new approach to health and disease. Modern Western medicine tends to be divisive, often looking at one part of the body without seeing its relation to the whole. Acupuncture draws together all the diverse signs and symptoms of ill health to form a basic 'pattern of disharmony'. This pattern will include the mental/emotional state as much as physical symptoms. These signs and symptoms are not regarded as problems in themselves to be 'eliminated', but as warning signs, pointers to imbalance in the patient. These imbalances can be corrected by inserting fine needles into specific acupuncture points on relevant meridians.

Acupuncture, then, stimulates the body's own self-healing powers and as there is a return to normal, the symptoms disappear of their own accord.

Nothing can ever replace the patient's own efforts to discover and remedy the causes of their illness. Acupuncture doesn't deny patient responsibility nor is it a panacea for all ills. But until we learn to live wisely, of our own accord, there is a need for helpers to point the way and for systems of medicine that help to restore the balance, without upsetting it. Acupuncture is grounded in the theory of traditional Chinese medicine with its practical and subtle understanding of health. With health understood, disease is put in context – health must be restored, rather than disease removed.

The aim of acupuncture is to restore the proper flow of Qi, the body energy or life force. This can be controlled at various points along the meridian system which networks the body. This is an ancient representation of the Small Intestine meridian, Hand Tai Yang, with the various points along it indicated.

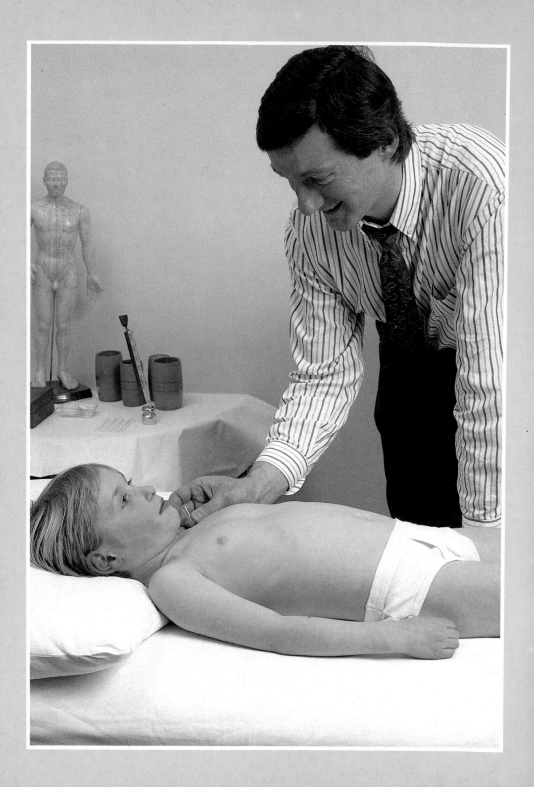

2

HOW CAN ACUPUNCTURE HELP?

An acupuncturist who returned to the West recently after undertaking advanced studies in China reported that Chinese acupuncturists are now seriously discussing a fundamental question. They are not simply questioning what new disorders their science can be used for, however, for this is not the Chinese medical perspective, which is person – rather than disease – oriented. But its use is so wide-ranging and widespread that the question now is rather when is it *not* helpful than what is it helpful for.

This implied boast shows the confidence they have in their traditional medicine, based on thousands of years of experience and study. This confidence is further reflected in the inclusion today of colleges and hospitals specializing in traditional Chinese medicine within – indeed as a major part of – their national health-care system. These colleges and hospitals place traditional practices on an equal footing with Western medicine, and the Chinese refer to this combination as having the advantages of 'walking on two legs', giving the patient the choice of therapy. It is interesting to wonder whether the Chinese – if they regard traditional and Western medicine as complementary limbs, equally important for supporting a healthy nation – are puzzled by the West's apparent determination to concentrate on hopping along on one leg only.

The holistic approach

In Western medical terms we are accustomed to thinking of diseases as more or less specific entities. Consequently we tend to judge the effectiveness of therapy in similar terms – it works if it gets rid of the disease. In the case of acupuncture, however, a different approach is required. An acupuncturist does not want to dodge the question if asked, can acupuncture cure cancer? Or can it treat arthritis, asthma, or psoriasis? But nevertheless he or she would prefer to hear the question expressed differently.

To an acupuncturist, such questions might present themselves thus: can the *Qi* which is so blocked as to cause the immobility of arthritis be moved again? Can the imbalance that is showing *through* the asthma be corrected? Or again, rather than asking simply can cancer be cured, an acupuncturist will ask whether a particular person suffering from cancer can be brought back to health – or, if this is unrealistic because of the extent of the growth, can their suffering be reduced?

It is also important to recognize that acupuncture is only one part of the whole spectrum of traditional Chinese medicine. This also includes treatment with herbs, diet, massage and exercise and at times these other methods of treatment may be used in conjunction with acupunture or even instead of it (see Chapter 6). Acupuncture is not, therefore, a system of medicine in isolation. It should be seen as one major method of treatment within a complete system that has a different perspective on health from that of orthodox Western medicine. As the holistic approach gains more and more ground in the West, acupuncture is becoming more widespread.

The common aim of all these traditional methods is to restore a person's health, balance and harmony on all levels – physical, mental, emotional and spiritual – by stimulating the body's own self-healing powers. The concept of holistic medicine, in which the person is seen as a whole rather than as a biological machine afflicted by a series of different symptoms, although relatively new in the West, has been familiar for a long time to the Chinese. In contrast, the idea of treating a patient's headaches in one medical department, their period pains in another, and their insomnia in a third, would seem to them extraordinary since there must be a common root.

A holistic viewpoint has always formed the basis of Chinese traditional diagnosis: in this, for example, asthma is just a disease label identifying a general theme – and people with asthma will all show different variations on that theme. In one patient an attack may be precipitated by excitement or stress; in another by exertion; in a third attacks may always occur at night. An acupuncturist would look at each patient's background constitution, and would find perhaps that one tends to sweat heavily, while another has very dry skin, and a third also suffers from eczema. Questions on their general health would also be asked – family history, digestion, diet, bowels, etc. to set the 'asthma' in context of that particular patient. The patient may also be asked about emotional factors, as to the Chinese, a family death, or other form of grief may be a contributing factor to the onset of disease.

All these apparently irrelevant features are important because acupuncture treatment concentrates on the whole person, not just the disease that has brought the patient to the acupuncturist.

Not surprisingly, it is much more demanding to practise an integrated viewpoint than to focus only on particular symptoms. In the latter approach, each symptom can be dealt with in relative isolation, whereas in the former all must be constantly related to the whole until the complete pattern of disharmony is corrected to re-establish health.

Although the holistic approach may be more difficult to practise, it is also more realistic in many ways. By taking in many different facets of a case as a matter of course, it gives a greater understanding of the patient's health as a whole, by providing a rounded and comprehensive picture. It emphasises the uniqueness of each individual and ensures that that *patient* is treated, not just some disease-label.

What types of illness can acupuncture treat?

In acupuncture, because the approach is holistic, you cannot isolate the condition from the patient. Also because it has a different diagnosis framework this is not really an appropriate way to assess the effectiveness of acupuncture. Nevertheless, it is difficult to show the depth and scope of acupuncture's potential action without using this Western perspective and without giving examples in Western medical terms.

Thinking within a Western framework, therefore, the following types of illness – some of which are diseases, some disorders, and some symptoms – indicate the remarkably wide range of conditions in which treatment by acupuncture has been effective.

Bone, muscle or joint problems – including: arthritis; backache; inflamed, injured or strained muscles; sciatica.

Cardiovascular disorders – including: angina; high or low blood pressure; stroke; thrombosis.

Childhood illnesses – including: catarrhal conditions; colds; coughs; earache; skin problems; teething problems; acupuncture is remarkably effective in the treatment of children, some practitioners preferring to use massage.

Disorders of the head area – including: facial paralysis; headaches; migraine; trigeminal neuralgia; vertigo.
Ears – including: deafness; otitis media; tinnitus.
Eyes – including: conjunctivitis; glaucoma.

Casetaking Many patients come to an acupuncturist for a minor problem such as backache or headaches because they have heard acupuncture may be able to help. They are pleasantly surprised to see the thoroughness of the casetaking and diagnosis and it is very common for patients to continue with treatment after the initial complaint has been resolved, either as a preventive measure or to help with other aspects of their health.

Mouth – including: gum and tooth problems; ulcers.
Nose – including: chronic catarrh; nosebleeds; sinusitis.
Throat – including: sore throat; tonsillitis.

Emergency conditions – needing hospital supervision and often combined with Western medicine – e.g. coma, convulsions, sunstroke.

Endocrine problems – including: hyperthyroidism; hypothyroidism.

Gastrointestinal disorders – including: constipation; diarrhoea; gastritis; duodenal and gastric ulcers; vomiting.

Gynecological and obstetric problems – including: discomfort in pregnancy and as an aid to labour; menstrual problems (amenorrhoea, dysmenorrhoea, menorrhagia); morning sickness; thrush (candidiasis, moniliasis).

Infectious diseases – including: dysentery; hepatitis; influenza; measles; mumps; whooping cough (pertussis).

Liver and gall bladder disorders – including: gall bladder inflammation (cholecystitis); gallstones (cholelithiasis); liver enlargement.

Mental/emotional disorders – including: addictions, depression, hysteria, insomnia, phobias.

Respiratory disorders – including: asthma; bronchitis (acute and chronic); cough (chronic).

Sexual problems – including: frigidity; impotence; spermatorrhoea; sterility.

Skin disorders – including: eczema; psoriasis.

Urinary disorders – including cystitis, incontinence, kidney stones, retained urination.

It is important to understand that no acupuncturist would make the unequivocal claim that any identified disorder could definitely be treated successfully, for two reasons. First, because treatment is not directed at the disorder itself but at the person as an individual – and all people are different. And second, because the names of the diseases, disorders, and symptoms given above are, to both an acupuncturist and to an orthodox practitioner, only a general classification – for instance, there are several types of eczema and many possible causes of diarrhoea or vomiting. Each case is considered individually and not in the 'disease-framework' listed above. The scope and effectiveness of acupuncture is dependent largely on the skill of the practitioner and the willingness of the patient to change. The practitioner needs the perception to assess the underlying causes that are giving rise to the disorder and the ability to re-establish the flow of *Qi* through acupuncture. The patient needs to be open to the idea of change.

In contrast, there are a number of misconceptions about the uses of acupuncture. One of these, commonly held by members of the public, is that it is only useful as an aid to giving up smoking or losing weight. Another, commonly held by orthodox doctors, is that it is only useful as a specialized form of anaesthesia in operations or as a source of pain relief in conditions such as arthritis. While it is true that acupuncture can be effective in all these circumstances, the reduction of it to no more than a limited 'technique' shows an ignorance of its potential that anyone with direct experience would find laughable. An equivalent misconception might be that modern Western medicine is limited to surgery on the one hand and the prescription of antibiotics on the other.

In summary, acupuncture is used every day in many countries around the world to treat people with both acute and chronic disorders, ranging from conditions of mild discomfort, such as a headache, to serious organic problems, such as gallstones. It may be used not only to treat back pain, coughs and colds or pre-menstrual tension, but also to influence the patient's 'Spirit'. To the Chinese the mind and the body are all part of one continuous whole, and both aspects may be affected with treatment. In all cases, treatment works by activating the acupuncture points, which stimulates the body's own restorative and recuperative powers so that the natural state of balance and harmony that is commonly called good health can be restored. An acupuncturist might say that treatment is analogous to removing a blockage to the natural flow of water, so that a stream can clear itself and run freely again.

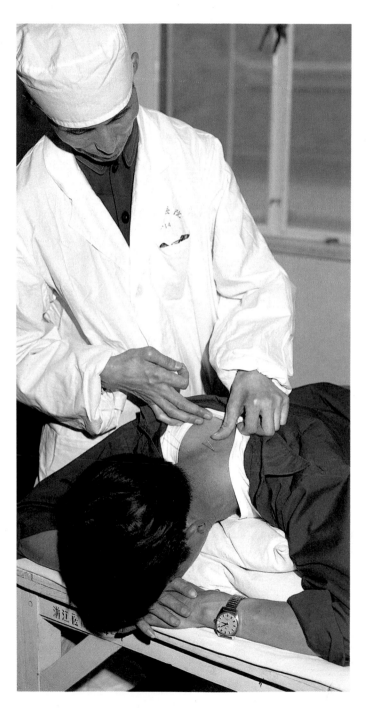

In China, acupuncture is regarded as a primary health therapy. Here an acupuncturist in a Hangzhou clinic feels for acupuncture points before treating his patient.

Short-term or long-term benefits?

The response of a patient to acupuncture is dependent on many factors. It depends most obviously on the severity of the condition and the length of time the patient has suffered from it. But the background history of the patient is also important. Factors such as general health, constitutional type, present circumstances, emotional balance, as well as factors such as the patient's diet and whether or not regular exercise features in the lifestyle, all combine to form the 'ground' in which the present complaint is rooted. An important additional factor is any medication the patient has received in the past or is receiving at the time of consultation, because this can have a significant influence on the ability of acupuncture to affect the patient's general condition.

It is impossible to generalize about how quickly or slowly acupuncture will work. Since acupuncture works with *Qi*, its speed is dependent on it, so children and those with good general vitality often respond very fast and those who are depleted or in old age may expect slower results.

Factors such as atmospheric pollution and long-term dietary abuse, combined in many cases with the persistent effects of conventional medication, are presenting modern acupuncturists in the West with a new and often troubling phenomenon, however. It is happening increasingly that at first the patient's symptoms seem to actually get worse for a time, as if the body is undergoing a period of clearing or cleansing during which toxins are expelled. The Chinese refer to this as 'eliminating *Heat* and *Poison*' or as 'resolving *Phlegm*', depending on the nature of the discharge. The process of clearing these problems properly may involve a temporary mild fever, sweating, skin disorders, and what is known generally as 'a healing crisis', before the patient starts to feel better. Thereafter, progress is usually fast, since the natural vitality of the body has been regained.

Some skin problems can actually be a manifestation of this attempt to clear toxins. Typically these involve redness and heat and some kind of discharge (the whole symptom picture is referred to as *Damp Heat*, in Chinese terms). Treatment usually leads to an initial aggravation, with more discharge and heat as the body is stimulated to throw out waste products and clear the blood. Dietary advice may also be offered to aid the clearing process. As treatment continues, however, the skin clears and the long-term benefits become apparent.

Back pain can produce a comparable reaction, with initial worsening followed by recovery and steady improvement. The combination of massage, moxibustion and acupuncture, however, can resolve the problem more quickly and strengthen the patient so that the long-term benefit is substantial.

Preventive medicine

The whole procedure of making an integrated diagnosis (which puts the complaint in the context of the patient's general health) is aimed at understanding the reasons behind the illness and then at resolving them. This almost always requires some independent effort on the patient's part. Furthermore, this comprehensive approach commonly results in problems other than the one the patient originally complained of being solved as part of the same treatment.

'A skilful doctor cures illness when there is no sign of disease and thus the disease never comes'
huai nan zi 120 BC.

A natural extension of this general health care is that, after treatment for one problem has been successful, patients return regularly – usually about every three months – for check-ups, to ensure that the initial improvement is maintained and that other problems do not arise. What kind of subsequent treatment may be needed, or how long it will last varies from case to individual case, because each patient presents a different pattern. Physical, mental and emotional factors make a great deal of difference to the ever-changing patient picture.

Such an emphasis on preventive medicine and health maintenance has always been a central feature of acupuncture and, indeed, Chinese medicine in general. By analogy, it is better to take care of a garden when the weeds are small, or even to prevent their growth in the first place, than to wait until they flower and spread their seeds. A passage from the foundation text of Chinese medicine, *The Yellow Emperor's Classic of Internal Medicine*, makes a similar point:

> *To administer medicines to diseases which have already developed and to suppress revolts which have already developed is comparable to the behaviour of those persons who begin to dig a well after they have become thirsty, and of those who begin to cast weapons after they have already engaged in battle. Would these actions not be too late?*

Acupuncture can deal effectively with many acute conditions as well as chronic ones, but it has the further strength of being able to spot the start of trouble – before the acute phase begins – by identifying the tendencies that could develop into illnesses. Treatment at this stage ensures that as far as possible everything can be kept on the best lines for optimum health.

Our attitude to health care in the West contrasts significantly with this, although in certain areas, such as general hygiene and public health, preventive medical skills are well refined. Those who follow a consciously healthy diet, or go for regular medical check-ups, are still in a very small minority, however. Most people would only think of visiting a doctor when they are ill. It could be that the contrast between the emphasis of Western medicine on quick results and that of acupuncture on long-term benefits is a direct reflection of this different perspective on preventive and maintenance health care.

How effective is acupuncture?

Much favourable research on the effectiveness of acupuncture has been conducted in both China and Japan. In the United States and Britain however less research is available partly because the scale on which acupuncture is practised is much smaller. Nevertheless some studies have been made in Britain, notably one by orthodox doctors in Oxford and another by the Consumers' Association, whose results were published in *Which?* magazine in 1986.

The Oxford study (see pp 40-41) showed that definite benefits were derived from acupuncture treatment of patients who suffered breathlessness as a result of chronic obstructed respiratory disease.

The Consumers' Association report drew attention to the fact that most acupuncturists are constantly seeing patients for whom orthodox medicine has not worked, despite extensive tests and treatment. The report found that acupuncture achieved a remarkably high success rate even in these circumstances. Additionally, many practitioners were quick to point out that, if the patients had come to see them earlier, the problems would have been much less difficult to deal with and the success rate even higher.

Acupuncture and degenerative disease

Acupuncture's effectiveness depends on its ability to improve the flow of *Qi* in the body. If *Qi* is very depleted, or if its flow is blocked, progress is likely to be slow or even

Acupuncture can also be effective as preventive medicine. In China, acupuncturists visit the work force in situ as a routine screening exercise. Here the acupuncturist checks the pulses of a worker in a collective. It is traditional to have a toning-up acupuncture session at the turning of the seasons, to prepare the body for changes in climate.

non-existent. In conditions of great depletion the patient's constitution must be 'built up' – traditionally with diet and herbal remedies – so that acupuncture can have an effect. In old age, treatment may take longer than is normal for younger people simply because the older body naturally has less vitality.

If a patient is unwilling to make changes to diet or lifestyle that the acupuncturist recommends, this may also reduce the treatment's effectiveness. Similarly, if a patient has been receiving medication from an orthodox practitioner, especially on a long-term basis, acupuncture treatment is likely to be difficult and take some time to be effective.

If the blockage or stagnation of *Qi* is very great, as it would be in a case where gross organic damage has occurred, as for instance in certain cancers, surgery may be necessary. In other cases, such as terminal cancers, where the condition itself does not respond to any therapy, it is nevertheless often possible to alleviate the patient's suffering to some extent through acupuncture. Although the patient's vitality may be low and the potential for self-healing therefore greatly reduced, acupuncture's ability to maximize whatever potential there is can only be helpful. The quality of his or her life can be much improved and helping someone to die with dignity is as important as helping someone to live.

A similar principle is important in the use of acupuncture to treat serious degenerative disorders such as Parkinson's disease. In such cases the patient usually comes to an acupuncturist when the disease is at a relatively late stage, and often after several years of medication. These circumstances certainly make treatment very difficult, but some benefit may be gained nevertheless, usually through enabling the medication to be reduced or in slowing the disease process. Comparable results can sometimes be achieved with diseases such as epilepsy although the extent of improvement will inevitably vary.

AIDS and acupuncture

Acupuncture is being used increasingly in the treatment of AIDS, but this is a recent phenomenon and it is difficult to assess the benefits in the long term. As with any treatment, effectiveness will depend upon the severity of the individual condition, the amount of physical deterioration involved, and what medication is being used.

In the early stages, acupuncture can be very helpful to re-activate the immune system, and at all stages can help to deal with the wide range of symptoms which tend to manifest. With re-balanced energy, the patient generally feels more relaxed and positive, maximizing the chances of a return to health. See also Sterilization, Chapter 8.

In the West, doctors tend to rely more on technology than the 'hands-on' approach of the acupuncturist. Even so, preventive medicine, an idea long established in acupuncture, is becoming more popular, and monitoring the healthy is now common practice in orthodox medicine. This is a routine blood pressure check.

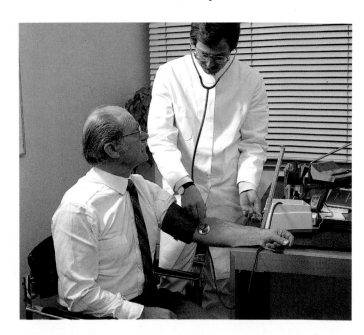

Tests have shown that many types of sleeping pills reduce the Rapid Eye Movement (REM) phase of sleep, which is the time when most dreaming takes place. All sleeping drugs tend to interfere with the natural sleeping patterns that are important for psychological stability. Withdrawal from these drugs tends to increase the Rapid Eye Movement phase, which can lead to restless sleep and excessive dreaming, often with nightmares. Acupuncture can be helpful in alleviating these unpleasant effects as well as helping to establish a natural pattern of sleep.

Sleeping problems

If a patient has problems sleeping, and feels unable to cope without sleeping pills, the acupuncturist can help to reduce the drugs, while assisting with regulating the patient's sleeping patterns. Dependence on sleeping pills may be physical or psychological, and return to normal sleep may take up to six weeks.

It is important to understand that sleeping pills have no direct therapeutic effect – they do not 'cure' in any way, but only alleviate the symptoms. If sleeping pills have been prescribed during a time of stress, it is essential that they are not continued to a point at which dependence, whether psychological or physical, can occur.

Tranquillizers and stimulants

Public awareness of the danger of mood-altering drugs has increased in the past few years. Recent attempts to curb spending in the British National Health Service has made the prescription of some named drugs more difficult. Nevertheless, the ease with which these potentially dangerous and addictive drugs are made available is still alarming.

To the acupuncturist, the prescription of tranquillizers and stimulants to treat cases of anxiety and depression is a cause of great concern. It is probably one of the most disturbing examples of the tendency within Western orthodox medicine to treat the symptoms rather than the cause of a problem. There may be occasional cases where the use of anti-depressants for a limited period may help the patient to cope with an overtaxing situation without apparent harm. On the other hand, an awareness of surveys linking extended use with ultimate addiction should make all prescribers treat any mood-altering drugs with extreme caution. Like sleeping drugs, which are classified in the same

The insomniac A middle-aged woman suffers from insomnia. She has been taking sleeping pills for the past six months, but recently they are not so effective and she is reluctant to increase the dosage. Further questioning reveals that she has occasional migraine headaches accompanied by visual disturbance. The acupuncturist diagnoses excess *Liver Fire* affecting the *Spirit*. Treatment aims to balance the *Liver* function, to calm the nerves and to quieten the *Spirit*. After six treatments, the patient is able to sleep without the aid of drugs.

category as the depressants or hypno-sedatives, tranquillizers and stimulants do not offer a direct cure, merely an alleviation of symptoms. Furthermore, their effect is usually only short-term.

With many mood-altering drugs, continued use brings about tolerance, and maintaining their effectiveness therefore requires increasing the dosage. A further danger is that, unlike heroin and the other opiates – in which an increased tolerance also brings about an increased resistance to the drug's toxic effects, (i.e. a dosage that can be used by a long-standing addict with no harmful effects, would easily kill a novice) – the toxicity of hypno-sedative drugs remains consistent. This means that if the dosage is increased in order to increase the effect of the drug, the possibility of accidental overdose is also increased.

Withdrawal from all kinds of addictive drugs can be helped by acupuncture treatment, although success will depend to a certain extent on the patient's determination and willingness to change.

Mind and emotions

Oriental – in common with nearly all 'alternative' – systems of medicine, stress the importance of the 'spirit' in their understanding of health and illness. To the acupuncturist, if the spirit (*Shen*) is not balanced, the whole system is lacking control and direction. It is just as important that problems of the spirit are treated by rebalancing, removing blockages and restoring the natural flow of energy, not by suppressing symptoms with potentially addictive medicines, as it is that those of the body are treated in this way.

In China, acupuncture is in fact used as much for emotional and mental disturbances as for physical. This is primarily because the Chinese do not distinguish between physical and mental problems as we do in the West: both are treated at the same time by the same doctor, and are seen as different manifestations of one pattern of disharmony.

Most patients find acupuncture treatment relaxing and calming and, in the longer term, problems of emotional imbalance can be treated as effectively as those of physical imbalance. Emotional imbalances, if untreated, may eventually result in physical symptoms, and are considered by the Chinese to be one of the major causes of disease. Emotions should be expressed freely, neither suppressed or over-indulged.

Smoking treatments

Some patients find that a course of acupuncture treatment causes them quite naturally to reduce or even give up smoking. Acupuncture treatment tends to make the system more sensitive to toxins, and may therefore naturally make a patient feel that smoking is repellent. For the more serious addict, there are special treatments, both to clear and balance the lungs and to help the effects of withdrawal. The patient must be committed to stopping smoking, however, as acupuncture treatment can only 'help' the nicotine addict – it is not a miracle cure.

Acupuncture in pregnancy and childbirth

In childbirth, the use of acupuncture can have two main effects: the more commonly known is that it can reduce pain; less well known is that it can stimulate the contractions of the uterus, which helps to ensure a healthy delivery. Reduction of pain without the use of drugs is of special benefit, especially to the unborn child.

In China, acupuncture is also used to treat certain problems that occur during pregnancy, such as excessive morning sickness, or malposition of the foetus. Traditionally, specific treatments are also given to the mother during the third and sixth month of pregnancy to aid the development of the foetus. In general, conditions that are conventionally treated by drugs, which could be harmful to the unborn child, may be treated by acupuncture during pregnancy, to avoid the risk of some damaging effect. Even so, in all cases intervention is kept to a minimum.

The limitations of acupuncture

Apart from limitations in the practitioner's knowledge and skill, and in a patient's willingness to heed advice, the most significant practical restriction is the need for a practitioner to be present in order for treatment to be given. In China this problem is ameliorated by prescribing herbal remedies to be taken between consultations.

In the West other limitations reflect the lack of practitioners. In particular there is a need for hospital facilities, so that severe cases can be monitored and emergencies dealt with effectively – both severe asthma attacks and emergencies such as appendicitis are treated by acupuncture in Chinese hospitals – and so that immobile patients and the chronically ill can be looked after and treated.

The smoker A patient comes to the clinic requesting acupuncture treatment to stop smoking. On examination, the practitioner discovers that the patient's energy is low and out of balance and suggests a few treatments to harmonize the *Qi* before the patient attempts to stop smoking.

Treatment aims to strengthen *Lung* function, and to harmonize the *Spleen* to avoid formation of mucus. After three treatments, the patient has more energy, feels more relaxed and finds it relatively easy to stop smoking.

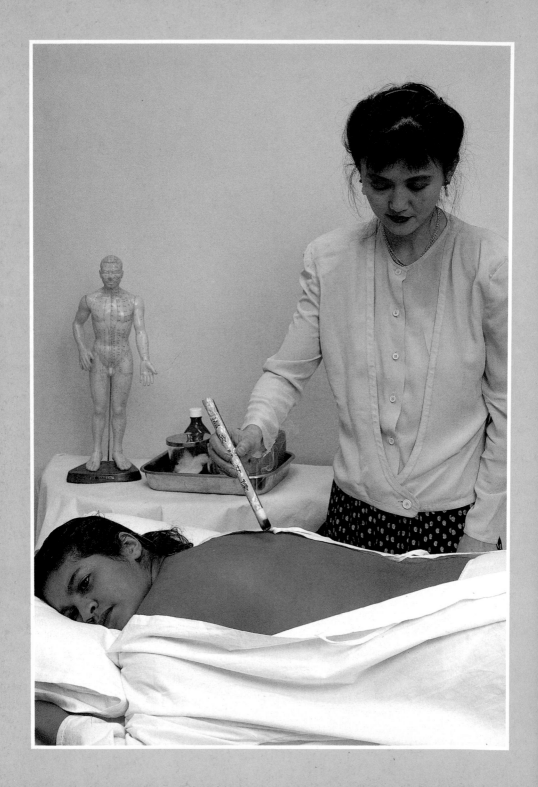

3

ACUPUNCTURE
IN CONTEXT

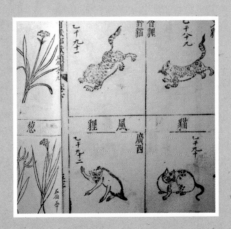

Although acupuncture is a long-established system of health care, and is relied upon by millions of people in China and elsewhere in Asia, it is still a relative newcomer in the Western context. And because of the importance of orthodox Western medical practice throughout the world, even in China, the relationship between acupuncture and orthodox Western medicine is an important and evolving factor in its future.

Before looking at this relationship, however, it is necessary to consider exactly what is the status of acupuncture today.

Modern acupuncture

Historically, acupuncture is a major part of traditional Chinese medicine. As such, it is intricately bound up with a unique theoretical system based on acupuncture points and meridians, combined with a theoretical and diagnostic framework that is completely different from anything encountered in orthodox Western medicine.

In China, the training for traditional Chinese medicine is five years of full-time study, two years of which are devoted to herbal medicine. Serious schools of acupuncture in the West have three-year full-time courses. Throughout this book it is assumed that only those who have undertaken serious study in China or in the West can rightly be called acupuncturists. This is a particularly important point for members of the public to understand, because they may be disappointed if they seek advice from someone with less thorough training.

An increasing number of family doctors are undertaking some short or part-time training in acupuncture. Although to some extent this benefits public and medical awareness of what acupuncture can offer, the inevitable limitations of these courses can have an unhelpful effect if they prevent an appreciation of acupuncture in its complete and integrated form. Commonly such pseudo-acupuncture concentrates on using acupuncture or acupressure techniques for local pain relief, and has little understanding of the central role of holistic diagnosis in traditional acupuncture.

Modern acupuncture, therefore, is neither more nor less than traditional acupuncture practised in modern times. It is this comprehensive and detailed system that is described in this book. Patients are advised to check that their practitioners have been fully trained (see p. 147).

Modern acupuncture and modern medicine

Where do these two systems meet? In broad terms it can be said, in order to characterize the distinctions between them, that acupuncture lays its primary emphasis on restoring and promoting health, whereas Western medicine lays its primary emphasis on eliminating disease. Although these could be regarded as similar aims, in practice the differences of attitude toward health and illness are profound.

For example, consider the treatment of a sore throat. More often than not a doctor will diagnose an attack by a type of bacterium or virus and will prescribe a course of drugs, commonly antibiotics, as treatment. The aim of the drug is to destroy the infection; it usually works and the sore throat 'disappears'.

The same patient consulting an acupuncturist is initially examined at length. The whole case is taken with details not only of the particular type of sore throat, its onset, development and present condition, but also the background to the case – whether this was unusual or quite common, general health, emotional state, etc. Let us say here as an example that it is discovered that the patient has been prone

This patient has a sore throat. After taking an extensive case history, the acupuncturist has decided that the problem is one of Wind Heat *and so has inserted needles on the* Three Heater *meridian at point 5, the* Lung *meridian at point 7 and the* Large intestine *at point 4. As with all acupuncture, the treatment is specific to this particular patient. Someone else may be suffering from a sore throat for other reasons, and their treatment will be different.*

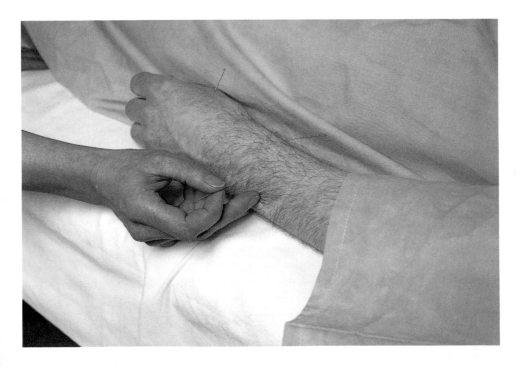

to sore throats since a year ago when his father died un-
expectedly. Since then he goes down with sore throats very
easily if exposed to draughts or cold weather. An acupuncturist might diagnose that the root cause was the patient's
Lung Qi being weakened with the grief at his father's death.
The *Lungs* are now unable to resist penetration by *Wind-
Cold*, which later turns to *Wind-Heat*. This has resulted in
the tendency to sore throats.

Treatment concentrates initially on the *Lung, Large Intestine* and *Three-Heater* meridians, with two objectives. These
are: first, to expel the *Wind-Heat* in order to prevent further
penetration to the *Lung* and to relieve the sore throat; and
second, to strengthen the *Lung* in order to improve its
ability to resist and overcome disease. In order to do this
successfully, however, the acupuncturist must assess why
there was weakness in the first place and then understand
how to rectify it. Through the strengthening of his *Lungs*
with further treatment, the patient is better able to cope
with the grief, moves through it and finds that he is no
longer prone to sore throats.

Acupuncture's aim is to build up the body's own, inherent powers of self-defence, rather than bring in outside
forces to help fight disease. By re-establishing the body's
vitality, treatment makes the patient fitter, stronger and
more resistant to future infection. Although antibiotics can
eradicate an infection, by doing so 'from outside', so to
speak, they may mask an underlying susceptibility and
actually weaken the body's ability to resist disease in future.
Most people who have followed a course of antibiotic treatment for a relatively minor infection are familiar with the
sense of weakness and debility associated with taking the
drug.

While orthodox medicine controls the symptoms of a
disease and may at the same time ignore the cause, acupuncture tries to focus on the root causes and relieve the symptoms as a consequence of this.

Another example might be a case of chronic arthritis. The
patient's ankles and wrists are swollen and hot; movement is
painful, and the joints are stiff first thing in the morning.

A doctor prescribes anti-inflammatory drugs, alternating
tablets with suppositories because of adverse side-effects
these drugs can have on the stomach. Treatment is aimed at
relieving inflammation, pain and stiffness and may be successful in this as long as the drugs are used.

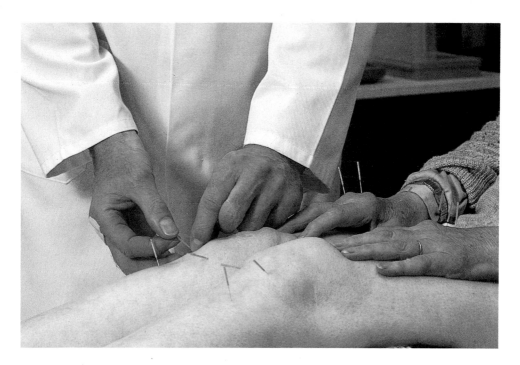

An acupuncturist assessing the same case enquires, among other things, about diet and lifestyle, and discovers a long history of lavish business entertaining, with substantial and regular alcohol consumption, combined with continual stress at work. Treatment concentrates on advising the patient to follow a much more modest diet and lifestyle, while attempting to reduce stress at work too if possible. Local points at the wrists and ankles are treated, as are points to clear *Heat* and remove stagnation of Qi. Diagnosis from the tongue also indicates excessive *Heat* in the *Stomach* and treatment is also directed to clear this. The medication is reduced, gradually.

Because the condition has been established for some years, progress is slow, and the joints often seem aggravated after treatment. Nevertheless, greater mobility is evident within a few weeks, the heat of inflammation diminishes, and the swelling slowly subsides. Changes to diet and lifestyle help ensure that the improvement is permanent. This example contrasts the long-term approach of acupuncture with the Western emphasis on more immediate (and symptomatic) relief as a step towards a hoped-for cure.

Acupuncture can help in resolving pain, without unpleasant side effects, for disorders which are debilitating but not life-threatening. Arthritis sufferers can often be helped in this way, with needles being inserted at various points, sometimes at the joints themselves and often elsewhere as well.

The dangers of drugs

An important stimulus to interest in 'alternative' therapies is the growing realization that the weapons supplied by a conventional pharmacopoeia in the fight against disease are all too often 'double-edged' swords. Most modern drugs have some side-effects, and some of these can be extremely severe. Penicillin can cause a severe allergic reaction; sedatives can become addictive; certain drugs that were approved as safe turn out to be potentially fatal; aspirin can cause the stomach lining to bleed; and the overuse of antibiotics has the alarming potential to encourage bacteria to develop resistant strains.

The list can be extended to other drugs used to treat various conditions, where prolonged use seems to achieve ever diminishing results, and may also cause ever increasing side-effects, even if these are relatively mild. Examples include the routine prescription of corticosteroid creams for eczema and other skin problems; inhalants for asthma; diuretics for reducing blood pressure; antacids to treat gastritis or even an ulcer; and tranquillizers for emotional problems.

To an acupuncturist, who often spends time having to clear up the problems caused by such long-term drug treatment, this approach seems almost unbelievably coarse and heavy-handed. It is frequently dangerous for the patient, and rarely seems to provide genuine long-term benefit. From a diagnostic point of view, suppression of symptoms produces confused cases, where the clues that should help unravel the problem have been modified or obscured. This makes the acupuncturist's job far more difficult than it needs to be – and puts the re-education of patients high on the list of priorities in treatment.

The medical view of acupuncture

It is an unfortunate fact that until very recently most medical doctors (certainly in England) were entirely ignorant of the true nature of acupuncture. They were also unaware of the extensive and specialized training required in order to practise it. And they were inclined to mock the risk-free benefits that acupuncture could bring to a great many of their patients. That there have been changes in this situation recently is to be welcomed. The Royal Society of Medicine in England set up a series of meetings between orthodox and alternative practitioners in the hopes of better mutual understanding. A survey taken amongst family practitioners in the Avon area showed many of them willing to refer patients. And in training medical students show an increasing interest in deepening their understanding of these alternative viewpoints on health and disease. In the USA doctors seem to be more aware of research showing the efficacy of acupuncture and there seems to be more openness to ideas of energy in medicine than in the UK. Here much of the early medical research was purely mechanical, ignoring the traditional theoretical framework and trying to explain acupuncture purely in terms of nervous impulses and chemical secretions, so leading to the idea that it was a useful technique for pain control and nothing else.

The public – more interested in results than theory – have been increasingly seeking acupuncture treatment (among other 'alternatives' such as homeopathy, chiropractic, naturopathy, osteopathy and herbalism) and this will in time undoubtedly lead to a more serious medical appraisal of this long-established system of medicine.

A more holistic approach to orthodox medicine is also gaining strength. In England, the British Holistic Medical Association has recently invited alternative practioners to become members and share ideas. In connection with this, moves towards long-term, 'patient-oriented' research in contrast to short-term 'disease-oriented' investigations will also tend to highlight the dangers and limitations of drug therapy.

From this new atmosphere of openness and willingness to consider alternatives could come a further development of the 'two-legged' approach found in China today. The strengths of Western medicine – especially in surgery, the fast response to accidents and intensive care – could be matched by the longterm benefits of the approach of the alternative therapies in which acupuncture occupies a major role.

Acupuncture and other therapies

Traditionally, acupuncture complements therapies involving herbs, massage, diet and exercise. In modern times this continues to be true, but acupuncture's relationships with other major medical systems – homeopathy and manipulative therapies such as chiropractic and osteopathy in particular – is gradually evolving. The following summaries of these therapies, as well as of herbalism as it is practised in the West, bring the picture up to date.

Homeopathy Acupuncture and homeopathy are two major medical systems that regard the 'life force', 'vital energy' or *Qi* as the key to health. They have much in common, notably a respect for the natural workings of the body, a belief in the patient's vitality or energy as a healing force, a holistic assessment of the patient, and an understanding of symptoms as indications of an underlying disorder rather than the disorder itself. Much good can come in the future from discussion and closer liaison between these two disciplines. Because they work in similar ways, however, it is usually best to be treated by just one of the two at any one time. Mixing them indiscriminately can quite easily confuse not only the patient's energies, but the practitioners themselves.

Osteopathic and manipulative techniques complement acupuncture very well. In China, massage is taught as a subsidiary subject to main acupuncture studies. In the West, acupuncture and osteopathic treatment may often be offered as mutually supporting therapies.

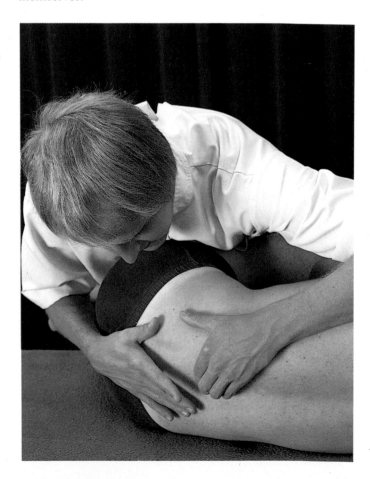

Manipulative therapies Acupuncturists in the UK frequently work in conjunction with chiropractors and osteopaths, and find that their approach to physical manipulation can be extremely beneficial where acupuncture alone is insufficient. Because of its ability to evaluate the energy or vitality of the whole person, acupuncture can also assess and resolve the background to a problem and so ensure that the improvement gained through manipulation is permanent. For example, a patient who tends to suffer recurring lower back problems, which osteopathy could relieve only temporarily, could find that concurrent acupuncture treatment reduced the need to return for manipulation. Massage is traditionally taught in China as an adjunct to acupuncture, and makes an excellent complement.

Herbalism Traditionally, the combination of Chinese herbalism with acupuncture has always been favoured, and many traditionally trained acupuncturists will have a working knowledge of both fields. Herbs are used especially to strengthen and build the body's constitution in deficient conditions. They have the added advantage that they can be taken at home, whereas acupuncture requires the presence of a practitioner. Treatment through diet and herbs combines well with acupuncture because the basic aims are the same – to restore vitality, clear toxins from the body, and restore health. Research in Europe and the United States is being conducted to see whether or not indigenous herbs may be more effective or more appropriate than imported Chinese ones.

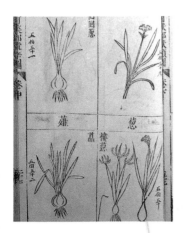
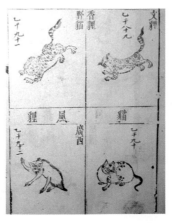

Chinese acupuncture is supported by herbal medicine, which is often used to complement it. Such medicines traditionally derive from both vegetable and animal sources, as indicated by these pages from an ancient Chinese pharmacopoeia.

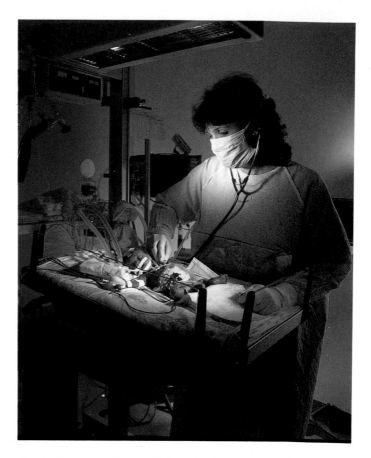

High-tech medicine as favoured in the West need not always mean unnecessary invasive therapy. Here one of the successes of high tech medicine, a Warming System, keeps a tiny premature baby alive by controlling the temperature around the child's body.

Orthodox medicine Although the relationship betweer acupuncture and orthodox medicine has already been dis cussed, it should be pointed out that, as with other thera peutic approaches, the relationship is constantly evolving At present orthodox medicine has vast resources of staff clinics, hospitals, training schools, and a massive support ing industry ranging from pharmaceuticals and plastics to nuclear technology and robotics. In contrast, acupuncture is practised only in a limited – although growing – number of private practices and co-operative clinics. Even though it has the potential to be a major alternative, therefore, the weight of numbers and lack of facilities force acupuncture into a subsidiary role at the present time.

This view is not intended to belittle the value of hospital services, with their superb patient-monitoring and life-saving skills, nor to deny the need for surgical and pharmacological care in accidents and emergencies. Nevertheless it remains evident that a large proportion of cases treated by orthodox medicine in the West are treated just as successfully – and sometimes more successfully – by traditional methods such as acupuncture in China without the inherent dangers of side effects from drug therapy. If medical care were to evolve in this direction in the West also, a massive burden (not only in terms of numbers of cases but also in terms of the costs of medicines and treatment) could be lifted from the shoulders of orthodox medical services.

Thousands of years old in the East, acupuncture is a relative newcomer to the West. Once its benefits as a safe, effective and inexpensive system of restoring and maintaining health are recognized, it will take on a major role in the health care systems of the West.

The proof in the practice

In February 1986, the British Consumers' Association magazine, *Which?*, conducted a survey of consumer attitudes to alternative or complementary medicine. They published their report, called 'Magic or Medicine?' in October 1986. The magazine originally asked nearly 28,000 of its members whether they had used any form of complementary or alternative medicine during the previous twelve months. About one in seven said they had. In May 1986, a more detailed questionnaire was sent to a random sample of those who had used some form of complementary medicine. The material in the survey was drawn from the 1,942 members who completed and returned the questionnaires.

SOME OF THE RESULTS OF THE SURVEY ARE AS FOLLOWS:

- 82% claim to have been cured or improved;

- 74% said they would definitely use this form of medicine again;

- 69% said that they would recommend this treatment to anyone with a similar complaint;

- 14% said the treatment was ineffective;

- 1% said that the problem became worse.

Although these numbers are impressive, the British Medical Association (BMA) does not recognize this kind of survey as proof that alternative medicine works. Scientifically, there is nothing to say that it was the specific treatment that helped the patient any more than a variety of possible external factors – or simply a placebo effect. The argument is that perhaps the benefits of complementary medicine are all in the patient's mind.

To attempt a more scientific or objective approach to the appraisal of alternative medicine, the BMA suggests that alternative therapies should undergo the same kind of clinical tests as orthodox medicine if it is to be accepted.

In order to find safe and appropriate ways of assessing alternative medicine in Britain, the Research Council for Complementary Medicine was established, and in July 1986 their first research project took place at the Churchill Hospital, Oxford.

The Oxford Research Project

The project was to study the effects of acupuncture on patients suffering from chronic breathlessness. It was a breakthrough for research in Britain in that it was conducted by a Chinese doctor, using traditional methods of diagnosis and treatment with traditional acupuncture techniques.

Dr Chen, from the Friendship Hospital in Beijing, treated 24 patients with chronic obstructive pulmonary disease. This particular disease was chosen by the Western doctors monitoring the project because it is fairly straightforward to measure results.

Dr Chen treated each patient individually, according to their particular presenting patterns of disease. Twelve patients received 'real' treatment, while twelve received ineffective treatment (although only two out of the twelve guessed that their treatment was any different).

The results were remarkable. Virtually all the patients receiving the 'real' treatment showed improvement, particularly in their ability to perform physical tasks without becoming breathless. These were all patients to whom the medical profession could offer no further help. Two of the control group also showed slight improvement, which was attributed by the team to Dr Chen's infectiously happy disposition!

The project received serious attention by the medical profession and was reported in *The Lancet* as well as in many of the national newspapers.

In Chinese medical terms the project was by no means perfect. It was conducted over a relatively short period of time and most of the patients were still receiving their usual medication. Dr Chen also pointed out that some of the patients would have benefited from treatment with Chinese herbs as a supplement, or in some cases instead of the acupuncture treatment.

Research in the USA

Although the Oxford project was a breakthrough in collaboration between traditional acupuncture therapists and the orthodox medical profession in the UK, in the United States this kind of work has a longer standing. The early research concentrated on the effectiveness of acupuncture for pain relief, but now many research projects are reported in the orthodox medical press on a wider variety of treatments with acupuncture.

In January 1987, the professional journal, *Obstetrics and Gynecology* printed a paper on 'Acupuncture for the management of Primary Dysmenorrhea' (menstrual problems) conducted by medical doctors in Oakland, California. It involved the asessment of 43 women over a period of one year, and included the use of three different control groups, as required to fulfil orthodox medical research procedure. In the group receiving 'real' acupuncture treatment, 90.9% (10 out of 11 patients) showed improvement: in the placebo acupuncture group, 36.4% showed improvement: in the standard control group, 18.2% and in the 'visitation' group, who received the least attention, 10%. There was a 41% reduction of analgesic medication used by women in the 'real' acupuncture group, and no change, or increase of medication in the control groups.

In 1980, the medical publication *Pain* reported a research project undertaken by the University of California Los Angeles (UCLA) and concluded: 'Acupuncture therapy, when properly administered, is an extremely safe and effective procedure which may be indicated for the treatment of certain chronic pain problems . . . Finally we recommend that its application for the treatment of pain be considered an accepted procedure, and no longer "experimental".'

The researchers also pointed out that their results, although positive, did not demonstrate the full potential of

Acupuncture is clearly not a panacea, but the sheer weight of evidence demands that acupuncture be taken seriously as a clinical procedure of considerable stature.

R.H. Bannerman MD reporting on the 1979 conference of the United Nations World Health Organization in the *American Journal of Acupuncture*, July 1980.

acupuncture because the requirements of the research controls prevented the full use of acupuncture techniques: 'In good Traditional Acupuncture a great many aspects of the patient's life may be changed at one time: not only are different points used at each treatment and at times moxa substituted for needles, but also the practitioner may make recommendations for change in life-style and diet.'

These problems of assessment have also been encountered by the RCCM in the UK and in 1986 a conference was held to discuss appropriate research methodology for acupuncture and other forms of alternative medicine.

Another line of research is that conducted by the University of Pennsylvania School of Veterinary Medicine into the effects of acupuncture in the treatment of animals. This is particularly interesting in that it rules out the commonly held belief that the effectiveness of acupuncture treatment depends on belief or the placebo effect. In fact this large weight of veterinary research helped convince the courts in Southern Texas that acupuncture does in fact work.

So, despite claims by both the American and British Medical Associations that acupuncture has not been proven to be an effective method of treatment, the increasing demand for acupuncture in the West really speaks for itself. The verdict of the US District court of Southern Texas in July 1980 (quoted in *The Journal of Traditional Acupuncture Vol. VI No. 2*) when considering the status of acupuncture was as follows: "Acupuncture has been practised for 2,000 to 5,000 years. It is no more experimental as a mode of treatment that is the Chinese language as a mode of communication. What is experimental is not acupuncture, but Westerners' understanding of it and their ability to utilize it properly.'

Research in China
Although research into the effectiveness of acupuncture is still in its infancy in the West, extensive research of a properly scientific nature has been carried out in China during the past 40 years.

When the People's Republic of China was formed in 1949, many of the revolutionary leaders were determined to rid their country of all religion and superstition, and to many of them this included traditional Chinese medicine. Others, although accepting the usefulness of Western medicine, felt that traditional methods should also be preserved. The story

is told that Chairman Mao became very ill while on the Long March, but his life was saved by folk medicine. He therefore supported its continuation, but also tried to ensure that these traditional forms of medicine would also prove valuable to a modern society by instituting a series of experiments and clinical tests, which were undertaken in the 1950s.

In 1958, after many thousands of tests, the members of the Central Committee were convinced that traditional medicine was effective, and since that time Western and traditional Chinese medicine have been given equal status in the People's Republic of China.

Chinese people can today enjoy the advantages of both traditional acupuncture and orthodox Western medicine. Chairman Mao initiated much research into acupuncture, which has helped to bring this medical system to the attention of the Western world.

Tests of this nature are still carried out in China. Medical publications that reach the West contain many well documented examples of the effectiveness of Chinese medicine in treating a variety of different problems. *The Journal of Chinese Medicine* published quarterly in Beijing for world wide circulation is dedicated solely to the scientific investigation of Chinese medical techniques, twelve or more projects being reported in each issue. For example, the Journal of June 1986 discusses the effects of acupuncture treatment for malaria, which took place over a period of four years. Of the 133 patients treated with acupuncture 111 improved and showed no signs of relapse after three to four months; blood tests showed that no malarial parasites were present.

In the same Journal, there is a report on the expulsion of gallstones using Chinese Herbs, and reports in the March issue of the same year discuss the effective use of acupuncture for the treatment of tumours in combination with radiotherapy or chemotherapy. This large body of research, undertaken by Western-trained as well as traditional doctors, shows an exciting way forward for the advancement of both medical systems.

However, the research criteria laid down by the Western medical professional tends, as we have seen, to restrict the type of acupuncture treatment that can be given – and also the assessment of its progress. Success in Western medicine is seen in terms of relief of symptoms whereas the acupuncturist measures success in wider terms. The aim of Chinese medicine is not merely to eliminate disease, but to change the functioning and quality of life. Patients receiving treatment will often comment that they feel better or are able to function more fully before any distinct physiological changes may be apparent. It is to be hoped that in the future, both in orthodox and alternative medical research, these important factors will be given a more central place and the patient seen as a whole being rather than in terms of separate symptoms.

Acupuncture in Western terms

We have taken a brief look at research into the effectiveness of acupuncture treatment, or 'the proof in the practice', which goes some way towards answering the question 'Does acupuncture work?' But the other main question of interest to researchers and laymen alike is the more difficult one of 'How does acupuncture work? What are its mechanisms? And how can we understand them in Western terms?

In 1971 an American journalist witnessed major surgery being carried out with acupuncture as the sole means of anaesthesia. He reported his observations in the *New York Times*, and stimulated a great deal of interest in the subject. Acupuncture was suddenly taken more seriously by the Western scientific and medical professions, and much research has since been carried out into the way acupuncture works.

Early research suggested a purely neurological effect (the 'gate' theory, or the reduction of pain sensations by the stimulation of other nerve pathways), whereas later research indicated the involvement of chemical mechanisms, transported via the blood stream.

Though this kind of research has gone a long way to assist the recognition of acupuncture in the West, it has tended to draw attention to pain control, rather than the more widely therapeutic effects and to ignore the theoretical basis of Chinese medicine, that of *Qi* energy, the points and the meridians.

There are, of course, exceptions to this and a major conference organized by the World Research Foundation called 'The Congress of Bioenergetic Medicine', was held in Los Angeles in November 1986. The conference aimed to 'bridge the gap between medicine and the latest discoveries in physics', and discussed, amongst other subjects, acupuncture and homeopathy. Particularly active in these areas of research are Professor William Tiller of Stanford University, California, and Dr Hiroshi Motoyama in Tokyo; both have been involved in serious scientific study of the body's subtle energy systems for many years. Dr Motoyama has invented a sophisticated diagnostic tool based on the flow of energy in the acupuncture meridians which is now used in hospitals in Japan, and to a much lesser extent in the United States, for early detection of organic imbalance.

The fact that this kind of research is still so rare shows one of the difficulties of uniting the Western medical world view with that of 'energy medicine'. That this is not simply a problem of Eastern and Western thought has been demonstrated by Professor Tiller's research into both acupuncture and the purely Western system of homeopathy. It is also a reluctance by the medical profession to accept the concept of subtle energy.

...our future medicine will proceed toward the development of techniques and treatments that can utilize successively finer energies.

William A. Tiller
Foreword to *The Science of Homeopathy*, by George Vithoulkas.

'Energy medicine' accepts the existence of a subtle energy system within the body, and believes that by affecting the body energetically, material changes can take place. Matter and energy are seen as interchangeable, in fact, energy and matter are seen as ultimately the same thing. These ideas are accepted in the post–Einstein 'energy physics', but the Western medical viewpoint tends to remain rooted in the old mechanical view of the world, which has shaped our view of reality for the past 300 years. This world view has taught us to see the body in terms of its component parts, rather than as a related whole; as a collection of individual organs and chemical reactions, rather than as a dynamic being: and possibly most tragically, as the mind as being totally separate from the body.

Of course this scientific method has had its advantages but as medicine advances technologically, we seem to be losing sight of the concept of health care, of the everyday maintenance of health and the promotion of well-being.

If we take a closer look at the basic concepts of the mechanistic view, and how it is challenged by the discoveries of the New Physics, we may find that acupuncture theory no longer seems strange and mystical but upheld by current scientific thought.

Medicine and science

René Descartes (1596-1650).

Modern Western medicine is based on what Western physicists call the 'mechanical' view of the world. This is deeply rooted in the seventeenth-century philosophical ideas of René Descartes (1596-1650) and the scientific theories of Isaac Newton (1642-1727). Both men saw the Universe as a great machine, perfect, mechanical and governed by precise mathematical laws of space and time. In medicine also, the body was treated as a machine, made up of component parts that could be taken apart and put together again. Disease was seen as a breakdown of the machine and the doctor's task was primarily to remove the disease, and if necessary also the infected part, sometimes replacing it with an artificial one or even (in recent times) a 'second-hand' one.

Descartes held that mind and matter were totally separate, thereby allowing – for the first time – research into the functions of the body to be totally separated from research into the mind. The mind was considered to be unresearchable, and so was ignored by scientists, who left its mysterious realms to philosophers, until the end of the nineteenth

century at least. According to Descartes there was 'nothing included in the concept of the body that belongs to the mind, and nothing in the mind that belongs to the body'. This convenient division of mind and matter allowed man to assume the position of a completely objective observer, and enabled him to understand the workings of the Universe and of the physical body simply by applying the basic laws of science, formulated by Newton.

For the next two centuries science strode forward in great leaps and bounds showing its understanding of nature, and its mastery over it. Medicine, using the same mechanical and analytical methods, discovered the intricate structural and later chemical components of the body – although medical research was generally on the dead not on the living.

Rembrandt's The Anatomy Lesson of Dr Tulp *was painted in 1632; it characterizes the mechanical world view that dominated the 17th century. The body was seen as a purely mechanical object, a set of disparate systems that could be dismantled and put together again without reference to the mind or emotions.*

The Copernican system outraged orthodox thought in the 16th century, just as the new physics is revolutionizing our outmoded notions today. Copernicus, the Polish astronomer, on the bottom right of the picture, proved conclusively if unpopularly, that the Sun was the centre of our Universe, not the Earth.

This view of our world as a machine – governed by the unchanging laws of time and space – and of matter, the basic substance built up of tiny atoms, held firm until the beginning of the twentieth century. There had been a couple of hiccups with the discovery of electricity and magnetism, neither of which performed in strict accordance with Newtonian rules, but generally everyone was happy to feel that we knew most of what was to be known about the workings of the world.

However, the quest for knowledge, once undertaken, could not be abandoned – and so this fanatical search to find the basic building blocks of our Universe also led to the shattering discoveries of modern physics. Discoveries and theories made over the last eight decades now seem to endanger the whole fabric of the scientific system from which they have emerged.

The New Physics

In 1900, the German physicist Max Planck discovered that Newton's laws could not be used to describe energy radiation. Although he tried to apply the hitherto reliable principles, they gave him some very strange results which were obviously untrue. The laws of classical physics did not seem to stand up when applied to energy.

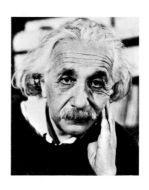

Albert Einstein (1879-1955).

A few years later, Albert Einstein made some interesting discoveries about the nature of light, and proved scientifically that light is made up of particles, or photons, which emit energy in small packets or 'quanta'. The only problem with this was that a hundred years before, an Englishman called Thomas Young had proved that light is in the form of waves. Both theories held firm, and in 1905 light could be described as particle or wave. This lack of certainty was to be one of the main pre-occupations of physicists for the next half century, and Einstein struggled with its implications until his death:

> *'What nature demands from us is not a quantum or a wave theory; rather, nature demands from us a synthesis of these two views which has thus far exceeded the mental powers of physicists.'*
>
> Albert Einstein

After the publication of the Theory of Light, which was many years later to win him the Nobel Prize, Einstein went on to publish his Special Theory of Relativity (summarized by the famous equation $E = mc^2$) which tells us that mass and energy are different vibrations of the same thing: in fact, we no longer talk of mass and energy, but energy/mass, and similarly, no longer of space and time, but of space/time.

Although most educated people can quote Einstein's theory in its shorthand form, very few of us have truly grasped the implications of it. There is good precedent for this. In the sixteenth century the Polish astronomer Nicolas Copernicus pointed out that the Earth was not the centre of the universe. It was not a popular theory and took centuries to make its impression on the average man. Similarly, Einstein's discoveries have yet to make an impact on our view of reality. Even the physicists working with these theories have problems in coming to terms with them. Albert Einstein himself likened the discovery of Relativity Theory to 'having the ground taken from under my feet'.

Recent developments

The next generation of physicists struggling with these con-
tradictions began to put forward the ideas of, 'uncertainty',
'probability' and 'complementarity' which now form the
basis of the new physics. They found themselves thinking
more and more about the philosophical implications of this
new world view: although these new discoveries had no
precedent in the science of the Western world, gradually a
number of modern physicists began to find correlations between their findings and some of the philosophical traditions of the East.

*In modern physics, the
image of the universe as a
machine has been tran-
scended by a view of it as
one indivisible dynamic
whole whose parts are
essentially interrelated
and can be understood
only as patterns of a cos-
mic process.*

Fritjof Capra
The Turning Point

*The general notions about human understanding which are
illustrated in atomic physics are not in the nature of things
totally unfamiliar, unheard of or new. Even in our own
culture they have a history, and in Eastern thought a more
considerable and central place. What we find is an
exemplification, an encouragement, a refinement of old
wisdom.*

J. Robert Oppenheimer

Chinese medicine has long assumed that energy and matter
are interchangeable.

*The Great Void cannot but consist of Qi (energy): This Qi
cannot but condense to form all things: and these cannot but
become dispersed so as to form once more the Great Void.*

Compare this with Einstein's opinion:

*We may regard matter as being constituted by the regions of
space in which the 'field' is extremely dense – there is no
place in this new kind of physics for both the 'field' and
matter, for the 'field' is the only reality.*

If we substitute the 'field' for the Great Void, we have a
curiously similar description. In his book, the *Tao of Physics*,
Fritjof Capra takes a detailed look into these correspondences, giving many examples of the correlations between
the discoveries of the New Physics and the ancient Chinese
view of the world. It makes exciting reading. Furthermore,
the fact that the book is an international bestseller suggests
that this reunion of ancient and modern concepts is an idea
whose time has finally come.

Acupuncture, physics and *Wu Li*

The Chinese term for physics is *Wu Li*, which may be translated as 'patterns of organic energy'. Acupuncture is essentially an energy medicine, acting on the body's subtle energy system to bring about changes in the mind and the body. In order to begin to understand it in Western terms we must accept the interchangeable nature of energy and mass, and of mind and body. We must also accept that the essence of nature is change and indeterminance.

That these theories are borne out by the world view of the new physics is exciting, but if the technology of this new science were to be employed in research into the subtle energies of the body, of the meridian system and the nature of acupuncture points, great advances may be made into the understanding of 'energy medicine'. In the past, equipment has not been available to detect these subtle energies, but in the near future, with the use of recent technological advances, a truly scientific verification of acupuncture may not be far away.

Orthodox medicine – despite its use of ultra-modern equipment and extraordinary feats in such areas as laser surgery and genetic engineering – is in many ways still deeply rooted in the mechanical world view. As the technology of modern medicine becomes more advanced, the treatment of patients has become even more dehumanized. The body is separated increasingly into component parts until we lose sight of the whole. The feelings and emotions of the patient are seen as having little or no relevance to the functioning of their body machine. Inevitably, patients are made to feel 'irrelevant' to their own cure, and are often actively discouraged from taking any part in their treatment other than that of passive receiver.

The Chinese system of medicine refuses to see the body in this mechanical way. If acupuncture's role in Western medicine is reduced to the treatment of local pain, as beneficial to its recipients as this may be, it is no longer Chinese medicine. Only in the context of its ancient philosophy can acupuncture be seen as a vital part in a comprehensive medical system.

Let us hope that our Western world view will soon catch up with the discoveries of modern science, and energy medicine will become more acceptable to the Western mind. Fortunately for us all, however, our bodies seem to be able to understand it quite well.

The fact that all the properties of particles are determined by principles closely related to the methods of observation would mean that basic structures of the material road are determined, ultimately, by the way we look at this world; that the observed patterns of matter are reflections of patterns of mind.

Fritjof Capra
The Turning Point

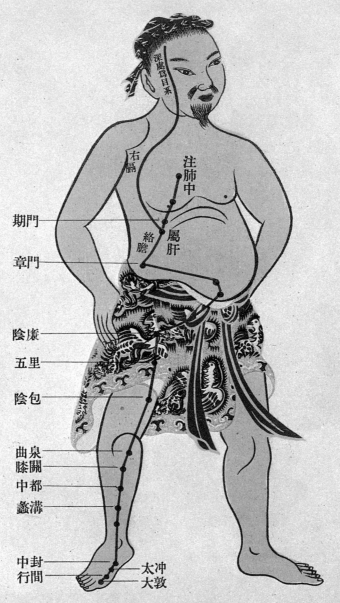

足厥陰肝經之圖

凡一十三穴
左右共二十六穴

深厚鶯目系

右膈

注肺中

屬肝

絡膽

期門

章門

陰廉

五里

陰包

曲泉
膝關
中都
蠡溝

中封
行間

太冲
大敦

圖 六 十——仿明版古圖（六）

4

HOW
ACUPUNCTURE
WORKS

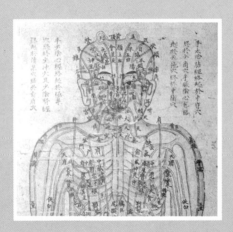

It is impossible to understand acupuncture without understanding Chinese medicine; and Chinese medicine can only be properly understood in the context of Chinese philosophy. This has always been a stumbling block when acupuncture is evaluated by Western scientific methods. The condensed account below is an attempt to clarify the philosophy for Western readers and show how it forms the basis for acupuncture.

Another obstacle to understanding is anatomical terminology, which can differ between Chinese and Western usage. To avoid confusion in this book, all words used in a Chinese – rather than a Western – sense are written in italics, in the same way that actual Chinese words are. For example, the word *Heart* refers to the Chinese term – which means more than just the anatomical heart we think of in the West.

Understanding the principles

Stripped of its cultural background, acupuncture may nevertheless be an effective way of treating certain conditions, local pain for example. But it is only in relation to the complex theory of Chinese medical philosophy that it can ever be used as a comprehensive medical system.

To begin to understand how acupuncture works, we must first examine some of the philosophy behind it.

Heaven and Earth

In the Chinese view of the world, mankind is seen as living between Heaven and Earth. The energies and influences of Heaven and the energies and influences of Earth intermingle within human beings in a dynamic balance. To put it very simply, the air we breathe – coming from Heaven – and the food we eat – coming from the Earth – combine in us to provide the energy necessary for life.

The body is seen as the dynamic centre for this interchange. But Heaven and Earth to the Chinese are more than just producers of air and food. They represent two poles – creative and receptive; an impulse and its manifestation.

This meeting of Heaven and Earth within a person must be kept in harmony and balance. Each of the internal organs has a particular function in this process, and must be able to work well and in harmony with the other organs. It is a finely tuned system, and breakdown in any one area will ultimately affect the whole.

The proper relationship between Heaven, Earth and Man has been a continual theme in all Chinese culture. Here harmony is shown in the rarefied mists of Heaven and the striking mountains and flowing rivers of Earth which all combine to influence the life of Man. For health and peace, this harmonious interplay must be maintained.

If too much energy is used, exhaustion follows. This is not the way of Dao. *Whatever is contrary to* Dao *will not last long.*
'Dao De Jing', chapter 55

The *Dao*

A central idea in Chinese philosophy is the concept of the *Dao* (also called '*Tao*'), which was expounded in the classic text called the *Dao De Jing* (more commonly known in the West as the *Tao Te Ching*). The *Dao* is the road, the path or the way, and consequently the way we do things, or the way the Universe works. To keep in harmony with the *Dao* is to live in harmony with the way that the Universe works – to keep in tune with nature and natural law. In Chinese medical terms, this idea of harmony amounts to a definition of health.

So how do we achieve this in the modern world? It seems

Big city pressures make it difficult to achieve balance and repose in one's life; but these pressures make such a balance even more necessary for a full and meaningful existence.

quite easy to imagine the Chinese sage in his mountain retreat living in harmony with the way of the Universe, but many of us live in cities with busy schedules, or find ourselves stuck in an environment with little to remind us of the way of nature. Too often we can not even find the time to stop and think about the flow of our lives.

Whatever our lifestyle, however, we must aim to create a balance in what we do: to balance times of activity with times of rest, to balance expenditure of energy with nourishment, times of excitement with times of quiet reflection. In Chinese terms, this means balancing the *Yin* and the *Yang* aspects of life.

Yin/Yang

Yin/Yang expresses a system of relationships, patterns and functions. Everything in the Chinese view of the world and of life is related to a dynamic balance of *Yin/Yang*. Everything has an inside (*Yin*) and an outside (*Yang*), a top (*Yang*) and a bottom (*Yin*), and there is continual interchange and communication between the two. Life takes place in the alternating rhythm of *Yin/Yang* – day gives way to night, night to day; a time of light and activity (*Yang*) is followed by darkness and rest (*Yin*). Flowers open and close, the moon waxes and wanes, the tides come in and go out; we wake and sleep, breathe in, breathe out. *Yin/Yang* is a constant, continual flow through which everything is expressed on the one hand and recharged on the other. They are an inseparable couple. Their proper relationship is health; a disturbance in this relationship is disease.

In medicine *Yin/Yang* is used to describe and distinguish patterns of disharmony. Within the body, the back is considered *Yang* in relation to the front, which is more *Yin*; the lower parts of the body are *Yin* in relation to the upper parts, which are *Yang*; the interior of the body is *Yin* in relation to the exterior *Yang*.

In distinguishing illness patterns, weakness suggests *Yin*, strength *Yang*; fast, sudden onset, suggests *Yang*; slow and lingering conditions are *Yin*; underactivity is *Yin*, overactivity, *Yang*.

The basic patterns of disharmony have been classified in Chinese medicine as the Eight Principle Patterns (see also p.91), and are grouped together under their basic *Yin/Yang* aspects: *Interior/Exterior, Deficiency/Excess* and *Cold/Heat*.

These terms are encountered again and again in Chinese medicine and provide one of the basic tools for diagnosis.

Many books give lists of *Yin* and *Yang* phenomena, but such lists can be misleading. The important point is that nothing is ever entirely *Yin* or *Yang*; everything contains the possibility of changing into its opposite. For example, the front of the body is *Yin*, compared to the back which is *Yang*; but, looked at in another way, the chest is *Yang* when compared with the abdomen, which is more *Yin*. Similarly, the skin is *Yang* compared to the blood which is *Yin*. On the other hand, the blood becomes *Yang* when compared to the bone marrow, which is more *Yin*, being deeper and more interior.

This intermingling, changing pattern of *Yin/Yang* is beautifully illustrated by the symbol of *Tai Ji*, the great polarity. All things have a *Yin* and *Yang* aspect represented here by the light (*Yang*) and dark (*Yin*) areas. They are in balance, but this balance is fluid and changing – a dynamic equilibrium between the light and dark, an interplay and exchange rather than a rigid, fixed, static quantity.

The small black circle within the light area, and the small

white circle within the black demonstrate that nothing is pure *Yin* or pure *Yang* and everything can be further divided into *Yin* or *Yang* aspects. It is this that explains the endless variety of all life, the uniqueness of each individual. This understanding of individual variations is crucial to acupuncture diagnosis and treatment. In modern scientific terms, a parallel can be made with genetics where the mother's (*Yin*) chromosomes combine with the father's (*Yang*) chromosomes to produce a unique combination in the child.

The symbol also demonstrates the interdependence of *Yin* and *Yang*. The light grows out of the dark, and the dark grows out of the light.

The satisfyingly simple symbol for Yin *and* Yang *the Chinese concepts of opposing unities. Light and dark embrace and intertwine in perfect symmetry, each side containing a small seed of its opposite.*

> Yang *has its root in* Yin
> Yin *has its root in* Yang.
> *Without* Yin, Yang *cannot arise.*
> *Without* Yang, Yin *cannot be born.*
> Yin *alone cannot arise;* Yang *alone cannot grow.*
> Yin *and* Yang *are divisible but inseparable.*
>
> Nei Jing

This is the principle of mutual support which can be seen in any relationship. Mutual support is complemented by mutual control. There is a counterbalancing of *Yin* with *Yang*, and vice versa, a natural tendency to bring things back to a norm. Western medicine would call this homeostasis and see it in terms of hormone balances and nerve impulses.

At the height of *Yang, Yin* appears; when *Yin* is at its greatest, it transforms into *Yang*. This transforming of each into its opposite is constantly seen in health crises – for example when a high fever 'breaks' into chills and sweating. There are well known cycles of a similar nature in cases of depression, where the patient swings from apathy and indifference to a dangerously false 'high' or mania.

These primary concepts of the natural flow of life (*Dao*), expressed through the dynamic interchange of *Yin/Yang*, are at the root of Chinese medicine.

> Yin/Yang *is the Dao of Heaven/Earth*
> *The common thread in the 10,000 Beings*
> *The father and mother of change and transformation*
> *The root and beginning of life and death . . .*
> *To cure illness one must search for the root*
>
> Nei Jing

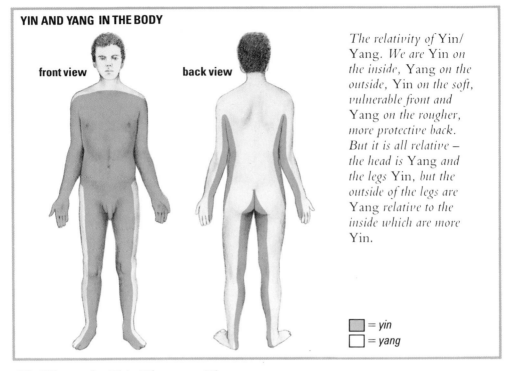

YIN AND YANG IN THE BODY

front view   back view

The relativity of Yin/ Yang. *We are* Yin *on the inside,* Yang *on the outside,* Yin *on the soft, vulnerable front and* Yang *on the rougher, more protective back. But it is all relative – the head is* Yang *and the legs* Yin, *but the outside of the legs are* Yang *relative to the inside which are more* Yin.

☐ = *yin*
☐ = *yang*

Wu Xing – the Five Phases or Elements

A further refinement of *Yin/Yang* are the Five Phases or Five Elements. Although not so ancient as the *Yin/Yang* concept, they have been a part of Chinese thought since at least 400 BC. The Chinese term *Xing* is difficult to translate exactly. It gives the idea of walking, one step then another, the idea of progress, movement, a living process, a stage in a cycle. It is commonly translated either as 'Element' which is perhaps a bit too static, or 'Phase', which lacks the idea of a particular quality. The problem is similar to deciding whether light is a particle or a wave.

The Five Phases are *Wood, Fire, Earth, Metal* and *Water*. Just as *Yin/Yang* represents a spinning unit of rest/activity, of dark/light, of inward and outward movement, so the Five Phases represent five different movements or aspects of energy, five energetic tendencies, five vibratory rates.

It may be easier to think of these in terms of the seasons. There are two *Yin* seasons (Autumn and Winter) and two *Yang* seasons (Spring and Summer) and their qualities illustrate the aspects of the Phases they are associated with.

Wood Spring is the time of budding growth, of expansion, of outward movement, of springing up, opening out. It exemplifies the qualities of *Wood* as a Phase – that initial bursting of energy, the rushing start of *Yang*, impulsive, full of movement and vitality. So *Wood* is activating, enlivening, free flowing, adaptable, creative. It is a quality that is seen in the unrestrained enthusiasm of children, or the first flush of Spring.

This quality of *Wood* can be felt in other areas apart from the seasons. In terms of compass directions, it is the East, the place where the Sun rises, where the day begins with keenness, freshness and renewed potential. In terms of climatic conditions, it is *Wind* – a shaking, trembling vibration, invisible but powerful. In terms of colour, it is green, the growing green of budding shoots. In taste it is the sharpness of sour things. In our bodies, it is the muscles and tendons which give us movement and flexibility. In the sense organs it is the eyes, which give keenness of vision and expand our awareness beyond the body. In the emotions it is anger, an excessive force of expression. In the Organs it is the *Liver* and *Gallbladder*, responsible for free flow and upward movement. Within the body this energy can be affected through the *Liver* and *Gallbladder* meridians with their special links with the genital region, the *Liver* and *Gallbladder* organs themselves, and the head – often troubled by migraine headaches, especially over the eyes, when this *Wood* energy is disturbed.

As *Wood* is a quality of energy, it is not limited to only one field of expression. This introduces another fundamental concept in Chinese medicine – the idea of 'resonance'. This idea will be familiar to musicians. Different string instruments tuned to the same note will vibrate when that note is sounded in the same room. The Chinese idea of 'resonance' extends this idea – different things with the same 'quality', 'Phase', or inner nature resonate in a similar way. In terms of Chinese medicine, it is the *Liver* and *Gallbladder* in us that are responsible for the qualities of Spring – movement and free flow of energy. Tense muscles, irritability, eye problems, period problems, digestive upsets or migraine headaches may indicate in broad terms disturbances of *Wood* energy or its governing Organs.

Resonance is probably the most difficult Chinese medical concept for Western minds to grasp. For this reason it is sometimes misunderstood, misused, or even dismissed by

Three ancients and three children gather around an unrolled banner that reveals the Yin/Yang *symbol of ceaseless change and transformation, the fundamental rhythm of nature and firm basis of Chinese medicine.*

TRADITIONAL TABLE OF CORRESPONDENCES ACCORDING TO THE FIVE ELEMENTS

ZANG ORGAN	FU ORGAN	DIRECTION	CLIMATE	ELEMENT
LIVER	Gall Bladder	East	Wind	Wood
HEART	Small Intestine	South	Heat	Fire
SPLEEN	Stomach	Centre	Humidity	Earth
LUNG	Large Intestine	West	Dryness	Metal
KIDNEYS	Bladder	North	Cold	Water

ZANG ORGAN	SECRETION	COLOUR	EMOTION	SPIRIT
LIVER	Tears	Green	Anger	Hun
HEART	Sweat	Red	Joy	Shen
SPLEEN	Saliva	Yellow	Obsession	Yi
LUNG	Mucus	White	Sadness, Grief	Po
KIDNEYS	Saliva (sometimes urine)	Black	Fear, Fright	Zhi

modern acupuncturists – especially those who also have Western medical training. Nevertheless it forms the basis of many important medical theories, including the function of the Organs and the effects of the climates and emotions.

Fire Returning to the Five Phases, *Wood* develops to *Fire*, just as Young *Yang* develops to Old *Yang*, or the growth and potential of the child develops to the full strength and maturity of the adult. Underlying *Fire* are ideas of a climax, the zenith, the crowning point, ease, accomplishment, abundance, a full radiant expression. It is expressed in the South, the place where the Sun rises to its maximum; in Summer, the hottest time of the year and the season of luxuriant growth; its climatic condition is *Heat*. In medical terms, it is also expressed as *Heat* inside the body, giving rise to swelling, redness and inflammation. (This is important in

TASTE	SEASON	BODY PART	OPENING
Sour	Spring	Tendons Muscles	Eyes
Bitter	Summer	Blood & Vascular Tissue	Tongue
Sweet	Between Seasons	Flesh (Shape of Body)	Mouth
Pungent	Autumn	Skin and Hair	Nose
Salty	Winter	Bones and Marrow	Ear

NUMBER	MEAT	GRAIN	PLANET	GENDER
8	Chicken	Wheat	Jupiter	Male
7	Lamb	Millet	Mars	Male
5	Beef	Non-glutinous millet	Saturn	Female
9	Horse	Rice	Venus	Female
6	Pork	Beans	Mercury	Female

differentiating between types of arthritic patients for example – those with hot swollen joints would be treated differently to those with stiff cold joints.) Its colour is red, the colour of *Heat* and activity – in medical terms this is often associated with *Excessive* conditions, for example the red faces of certain hypertensive patients in whom the *Yang* rises too easily, unrestrained by the *Yin*. In the body it is the red blood, fiery liquid of life that nourishes and maintains, distributed by the *Heart* itself – for the Chinese the ruler of all the Organs, and seat of the Spirit. The emotion associated with *Fire* is joy, fullest expression of the light and radiance of the *Fire* Phase.

Metal Following the seasonal analogy, after the height of Summer comes the Autumn – or, in the more appropriate American term, the Fall. The Phase here is *Metal*, symbol of contraction, condensation, movement toward the centre, a withdrawal that keeps only that which is most precious. After the splendour of Summer come the falling leaves, the fruits that ripen and drop, the seeds that set in the Earth in anticipation of the coming year. There is a decline of *Yang* and an increasing emphasis on *Yin*. It is the time of Young *Yin* when everything external is cast off and the internal is developed.

As Autumn heralds the end of the year, so *Metal* is seen in the West, the place where the Sun sets, the light declines, the darkness begins, and *Yin* dominates. The Fall contrasts with the upward movement and vitality of Spring. Its contractive quality is seen in the climatic condition of *Dryness*, in the season exemplified by withdrawing sap and withering leaves and fruits. The colour is white – the colour of death for the Chinese – also seen in the pale complexion of those with lowered vitality. The Organ is the *Lungs* – Organ of balance, rhythm and regulation, responsible in the Chinese system for causing the *Qi* to descend. The *Lungs* in turn are associated with the nose – first entry point of the breath that fills them, and with the skin and body hair. The emotion is sadness, turning inward on itself.

Water From Autumn, the seasons turn again to the last quarter, Winter – or is it the first? Here all seems withdrawn, when seen from above, but is secretly active below. The frozen end of the year, a time of rest, darkness and stillness. But this quiet period is also characterized by recharging, and regeneration – essential groundwork that provides the foundation of the forthcoming year. Is Winter more like a tomb or a womb?

This is the time of Old *Yin*, the full development of that receptive, nourishing, all-producing power of life symbolized by *Water*. *Water*, which surrounds land on Earth, gives life to crops, feeds, sustains, cleans and cleanses – it is the fluid medium of life. As *Fire* is linked to the South, to light and brilliance, so *Water* is linked to the North, place of darkness – where the Sun never shines – the hub of the stars, centre of the night sky. It is the hidden origin of life, mysterious, dark, unseen, obscure – the same quality that lies concealed deep in the centre of a seed, which is also expressed for all to see in the flower. This play between *Fire* and *Water* – expressed in the endless interaction of the phoenix and the dragon represented on countless Chinese objects from jewellery boxes to temple doors – is the archetypal interchange of *Yin* and *Yang*, the transforming basis of all life. The cold wasteland of Winter is the door to the New Year. From the death of everything above the ground comes the possibility of renewal below.

This is the base line of life – foundation, root and source – so the reproductive system is governed by this Phase which comes under the influence of the *Kidneys* (as seen by Chinese medicine). In the body, this idea of a solid foundation is seen in the bones – the whole skeletal structure – and within it the marrow that nourishes the blood. All the deepest aspects – fluid balance, hormonal equilibrium, reproduction – are linked with *Water*, the primal Phase.

Earth The four 'Phases' seen in the actions of Spring, Summer, Autumn, Winter – *Wood, Fire, Metal, Water* – represent qualities of movement, stages in a cycle, expressions of pat-

SHOWING THE FOUR DIRECTIONS WITH EARTH AS CENTRE

fire
south
summer
old yang
upwards
heart
small intestine

wood
east
spring
young yang
expansion
liver
gall bladder

earth
centre
inter season
stillness
spleen
stomach

metal
west
autumn
young yin
contraction
lung
large intestine

water
north
winter
old yin
downwards
kidneys
bladder

tern. They are completed by the fifth, central Phase, *Earth*, the place of change and transformation, the pivot, or the hub of the wheel.

As *Water* is the primal Phase, concerned with origin, source and supply, so *Earth* is the maintainer and preserver from day to day. All the seasons take place on *Earth*, and their effects can be seen through the *Earth*. The central point of the four quarters is the place of neutrality, of balance, of exchange and interchange. The Organs of change and transformation are the *Stomach* and *Spleen*, responsible for the breakdown and distribution of food products. In simple terms, being overweight or underweight might be an *Earth* problem in Chinese medicine and an acupuncturist might well work on the *Spleen* in order to correct it.

At this point, one of the particular difficulties of direct communication with Western medicine becomes obvious. Of all the Organs, the Chinese use of the term *Spleen* is most at variance with Western anatomical understanding of the same term. When a Western doctor hears a description of the Chinese concept of the *Spleen* he cannot connect this with his understanding of the functions of the human spleen as identified by conventional anatomy and physiology. However, there is no ready alternative to the Chinese term, so we need to be aware of this important differentiation.

Relationships between the Five Phases
Just as everything is *Yin/Yang* in movement and can be expressed in terms of *Yin* and *Yang*, so in a broader sense, everything is contained in the Five Phases and can be expressed in terms of them.

Chinese medicine is based on observation of qualities and this is extended without difficulty to Organs and parts of the body themselves. Everything is seen in terms of interrelating movements – is the *Earth* weak? Is the *Wood* too strong? Anyone who has been to a traditional acupuncturist will be familiar with their problems being assessed and described in these terms.

Before leaving the Five Phases it must be emphasized that just as nothing is just *Yin* or just *Yang* and it is the interrelationship and balance that is important, so with the Five Phases, the ways they move together and integrate in a person is the essential question. Their interaction is governed by definite relationships, known as the *Sheng* and *Ke* cycles. *Sheng* means to promote or engender. In the *Sheng* cycle

HOW THE ORGANS RELATE TO THE SHENG AND KE CYCLES

each Phase gives birth to the one succeeding it. So *Water* produces *Wood*, *Wood* produces *Fire*, *Fire* produces *Earth*, *Earth* produces *Metal* and *Metal* produces *Water*.

Ke means restraint or control. In the *Ke* cycle each Phase controls the next but one following it. So *Water* controls *Fire*, *Wood* controls *Earth*, *Fire* controls *Metal*, *Earth* controls *Water* and *Metal* controls *Wood*.

For balance and harmony both relationships must operate – if there is production without limit there is the danger of over-expansion. If there is excessive control without expansion there is the danger of restriction and stagnation.

In health, as in life, according to Chinese philosophy, mutual production and mutual control operate together smoothly and continuously. In illness, the proper relationships break down. So if *Water* becomes weak, it cannot nourish *Wood*, nor control *Fire*. If *Wood* is too strong it will overflow to *Fire* and restrict *Earth*. These are the principles by which different energies interrelate.

The Chinese view of the Organs links their disturbance to physical symptoms. *Wood* in the body is the powerful, free flow of *Qi* that is associated with the *Liver*. If this gets out of control it will invade and restrict the calm, centred, transforming power of *Earth* associated with the *Stomach* and *Spleen*. This combination of symptoms (and this explanation of them) is quite common in stressful situations that lead to anger and irritability which in turn will affect first the appetite and then digestion itself.

Cycle of Creation

– – – ▶ – – – = **SHENG**

Cycle of Control

──────▶ = **KE**

Key	
HT	heart
SI	small intestine
HG	heart governer
TH	three heater
SP	spleen
ST	stomach
LU	lung
LI	large intestine
KID	kidney
BL	bladder
LIV	liver
GB	gall bladder

The Chinese compass places the South at the top. The compass is no mere navigational instrument; apart from the directions, this one also shows the Eight Trigrams, the Twelve Earthly Branches and the Twenty-Four Solar Periods among other features. These divisions are all part of the way in which ancient Chinese philosophy explains the changing flow of life.

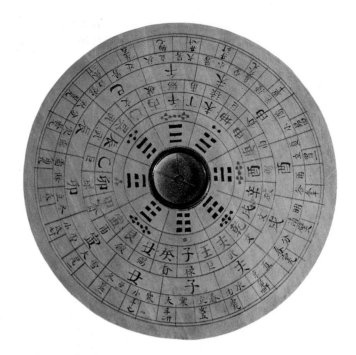

Further refinements

Yin/Yang and the Five Phases are essential to the Chinese world picture, but they do not stand alone. Further ways of cutting the same cake produce other methods of analysis in Chinese terms – the Six Divisions, the Eight Trigrams, the Ten Heavenly Stems, the Twelve Earthly Branches, the Twenty-four Solar Periods, to name but a few.

Volumes have been written on these aspects by scholars in dynasty after dynasty as the Chinese refined their understanding of *Qi*/energy and its different qualities. In this, medicine (the study of Man) was seen as just one branch of the whole study of Nature – which when looking up is also the study of the Heavens and when looking down is also the study of the Earth. Everywhere the same principles were found, manifest in different ways, and a discovery in one field could be used by analogy in another.

This seems likely to occur again as the discoveries – and implications – of modern physics meet the poetic images of the ancient Chinese world view. The map that will help to chart the 'field' – to use a physicist's term – already exists in the old Chinese compass that analyses in depth the different qualities of *Qi*/energy in the full circle.

Fortunately, for an overview of the system, we can stick to fundamentals: that the unity is in the *Dao* – a ceaseless natural flow; that this unity must manifest itself through *Yin/Yang* – upper/lower, outside/inside, dark/light and so on; that further division of this unity produces the Five Elements or Phases, five keynotes or qualities that can be seen in all things and under which the Organs and parts of the body are classified in medicine, as shown in the Tables of Correspondences.

Man as a pattern of energy

Acupuncture works by affecting the *Qi*/energy and Man is seen as an energetic being. The Chinese have always been keen on reducing things to their most essential parts. Matter is just vibrating energy, according to Einstein's formula ($E = mc^2$); by affecting that vibrating energy at key points (acupuncture points) you will affect matter.

The Chinese conception of the human body is unique in the completeness of its theory and the everyday application of that theory to the restoration of health through acupuncture. The biomechanical model of the human body – an assortment of mechanical and chemical reactions which, in illness, can be adjusted through the use of chemical drugs – is a restricted view of a complex, vital being. It is a legacy from the 'rationalism' of 17th-century European thinking, similar to the old-fashioned reductionist view of the 'clockwork universe', which modern science has left behind.

The Three Treasures

Jing, Qi and *Shen* are the Three Treasures of the five fundamental 'substances' with which Chinese medicine is constantly concerned – the other two being *Blood (Xue)* and *Body Fluids (Jin-Ye)*. A brief study of these is necessary before looking at the Organs, meridians and points.

> *The Three Treasures of the body are essence* (Jing), *breath/energy* (Qi) *and spirit* (Shen). *Illuminated and clearsighted intuition is* Shen, *that which penetrates everywhere and moves in circles is* Qi, *the humours and liquids which impregnate the body are* Jing. Shen *governs and controls*, Qi *presides over the application of orders*, Jing *presides over transformation and generation*.
>
> Commentary on *The Heart Seal Sutra*
> by Lu Qian Xu

Shen

Like so many aspects of Chinese medicine, *Shen* is easier to see and understand from its effects than it is to define. *Shen* is what gives brightness to life – in a word, the Spirit. It is concerned with radiance, a depth of being – it leads life. It also covers a broad field – spiritual awareness, consciousness and the mental faculties. It is overclouded in conditions of depression or apathy, disturbed in conditions of shock, displaced in mania, madness or delirium. It is linked with the *Heart*.

Qi

All things have *Qi*, are *Qi*, and are expressions of *Qi*. If life is movement, *Qi* is what makes things move and is the movement itself. It is activating, enlivening, animating. Without this movement, vibration, activity, circulation, and flow there is no life. These may be difficult ideas for the Western mind accustomed to thinking of matter and energy as separate entities, in spite of evidence to the contrary from modern physics. In the Chinese conception the energy/matter split does not exist. Living things are not seen as matter activated by energy, but as energy organized into matter.

Acupuncture works by modifying *Qi* via needles inserted at one or more of the 'tuning' points. Continuing the musical analogy, acupuncture works by changing the note, which is to change the quality of the *Qi*. It is effective at the same level as *Qi*, which is subtle, light, energetic and invisible.

Qi has specific functions, can be differentiated into different types, and is seen as flowing in the *Jing-Luo* – an invisible network of meridians and interconnections that integrates the whole energetic functioning of the body.

The principal functions of *Qi* are to activate and move; to nourish; to protect; and to warm.

Qi activates/moves: This primary function of *Qi* can be seen in all movements whether involuntary – such as heartbeat and respiration – or voluntary – such as eating, speaking, walking, and even thinking. Life is movement and *Qi* governs it. Much of acupuncture is concerned with restoring free movement and the proper direction of such movement. The Organs each govern definite aspects of movement – for instance, *Stomach* downward, *Spleen* upward, *Liver* free-flowing.

Qi nourishes: Although nourishment is more a function of *Blood,* Qi also nourishes and maintains the Organs and tissues.

Qi protects: A very important aspect – where there is inner vitality, illness cannot take root. Associated with this function is the role of Qi in increasing resistance to disease and strengthening the immune system as a whole. Acupuncture works to tonify and activate the Qi and is therefore important in the whole field of true preventive medicine – building up the body and its natural resistance so as to actively prevent disease.

Qi warms: We are warm-blooded and warmth is necessary for life. Qi produces this warmth through its activity, much as running a car engine will warm it up. Lack of warmth implies lack of life.

The Chinese divide Qi into various kinds, which are active in different parts of the body and are related to specific organs. So there is an *Original* Qi related to the *Kidneys* and the lower back and responsible for the strength of the constitution; a *protective* Qi related to the *Lungs,* which flows on the surface of the body; and a *nutritive* Qi that circulates continuously in the meridians.

Assessment of the strength of these different aspects of Qi helps an acupuncturist decide which points to choose for treatment which will restore harmony and balance.

Jing

The third of the Three Treasures that compose Man is *Jing,* which means essence, and specifically a refined essence. Within the triad, *Shen* is the governing Spirit; *Qi* the invisible mover without which life grinds to a halt; and *Jing* is the power of the seed, the secret of growth, development and reproduction.

Jing oversees our transformation from a fertilized egg, through embryo, fetus, baby, child, and finally from puberty to adulthood. It governs to a large extent the base line of our health – our constitution. It also governs our ability to reproduce.

Disorders of *Jing* are severe – problems of growth and development, inherited disorders, sterility and infertility. It is related to the *Original* Qi and linked to the *Kidneys.*

The Five Substances

Apart from the Three Treasures, two other 'substances' are important for Chinese medicine, *Blood* and *Body Fluids*.

Xue (Blood)

Blood is seen as a dense form of *Qi* whose primary function is to nourish the whole of the body. Together they form an inseparable couple in which the state of the one will affect the other. The relationship between *Qi* and *Blood* in the body is one of the best examples of the workings of *Yin* and *yang*. *Qi* is called the commander of the *Blood*. This is partly because of the role it plays in the formation of *Blood*, and partly because the Chinese consider that it is the *Qi* that causes the *Blood* to move around the body. *Blood* is called the mother of *Qi*, providing nourishment to all parts of the body. In acupuncture treatment, it is often symptoms relating to the balance of *Qi* and *Blood* that are monitored.

Jin-Ye (Body Fluids)

An important aspect of Chinese medicine, the *Body Fluids* have the function of moistening and lubricating. They are divided into two types. The *Jin*, thin and watery, are responsible for the moistening of skin and hair. The loss of *Jin* in excessive sweating is considered very depleting. The *Ye*, thicker and heavier, lubricate the joints, sense organs, brain and spinal cord. These *Fluids* are often affected in arthritic conditions, and if they are depleted there may be cracking of the joints and pain in movement.

As with *Yin/Yang* and the Five Phases, here also it is interaction that is important: the balance of *Jing* and *Shen*; the equilibrium between the *Qi* that moves and the *Blood* that nourishes; the proper movement and distribution of the *Fluids*. It is a dynamic, active, living system. This equilibrium is maintained by the *Zang-Fu* - the Organs and the ways they function. The functions of the *Zang-Fu* are integrated through the whole body by the *Jing-Luo*, the meridian network.

Zang-Fu (the Organs)

The Chinese concept of the *Zang-Fu* is based on an appreciation of the movement behind things – the realization that ultimately everything works in a similar pattern. The Organs represent the detailed working of that pattern in us.

It is more useful to think of them as zones of activity

rather than anatomical organs. Chinese medicine is more concerned with the Organs' function and spheres of influence than with their physical structure. These spheres of influence are much wider than the Western view of their literal physiological function.

The Chinese have two terms to describe the Organs, the *Zang* and the *Fu*. The *Zang* are the solid organs of the *Heart, Liver, Spleen, Lungs,* and *Kidneys,* and are *Yin.* The *Fu* are the hollow organs which make up the alimentary canal, the *Stomach, Small Intestine, Large Intestine, Bladder, Gallbladder* and *Three Heater;* they are *Yang.* The *Zang* are considered *Yin* because they store and preserve precious substances and govern the innermost workings of the body, whereas the *Fu* are *Yang,* because they are sites of activity and movement and are involved with the transformation of impure substances. An acupuncturist's concern is always with the integrated functioning of *all* the Organs. If one Organ is disturbed, then the acupuncturist will look at how it relates to the others; often another Organ may be treated to support it. Here the *Sheng* and *Ke* relations within the Five Phases cycle become important (see p.67): if *Fire* is too strong it may be *Water* that needs treating.

A thumbnail sketch of each *Zang* Organ will help to explain an acupuncturist's approach.

The Heart (*Xin*)

Traditionally known as the 'Master of the *Zang* and the *Fu*', and 'The place where the *Shen* resides', the *Heart* is considered to be the most precious of the *Zang* and, as the residence of the Spirit, the ruler of the *Zang* and *Fu*.

The *Heart* commands the *Blood* and the energy pathways, bringing nourishment, irrigation and the spark of life to each cell of the body. The state of the *Heart* is reflected in the complexion: a pale dull face indicates deficiency of *Heart Qi*; purple shows stagnation; redness, excess *Heart Yang*.

In traditional texts, the *Heart* is often described in its purely spiritual function of 'housing the *Shen*' and it is said that the *Heart* must be as a void, in order to allow the *Shen* to come and go and circulate freely. Chinese meditation techniques aim to 'empty the *Heart*', to bring about a state of peaceful equanimity. The loss of this quiet centre from which all life is governed is seen in many mental/emotional disorders where people just become a bundle of reactions without the calm stability of the *Shen*.

Heart A woman in her late 50s, who lost her husband three years before, comes for depression. She is still on a repeat prescription of the tranquillizers pre-scribed to tide her over at the time. She is subject to great mood changes – at times sitting on her own, feeling apathetic and depressed, at others becoming 'hyped up' and hysterical. The acupunctu-rist diagnoses an in-stability of the *Shen*, not being housed in the *Heart.* Treatment is directed to reducing the tranquillizers, clearing their effects and restoring tranquillity to the *Shen*, mainly with *Kidney, Heart* and *Liver* points. The tranquillizers are slowly reduced, the patient's vitality restored and she finds it easier to manage her new situation without her husband.

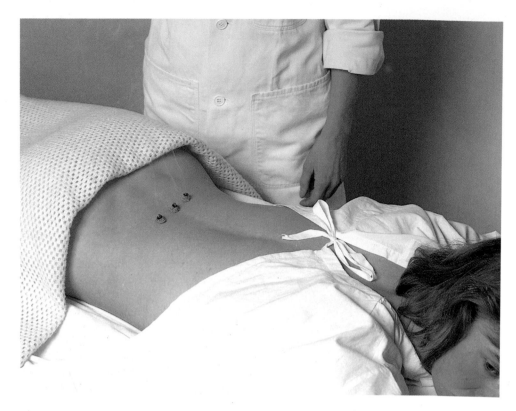

The strength of the Kidneys underpins the strength of the body's constitution, and so stimulation and tonifying of the Kidneys is often prescribed to supplement other treatment or used as a tonic. Here moxa cones are being burnt to tonify Kidney Yang and the fire of 'Ming Men'.

The *Heart* rules the *Tongue* – Organ of speech and intelligent communication. This is affected in manic depressive cases, for example, in which periods of great apathy, withdrawal and silence are followed by a hyperactive, extrovert, manic phase. An acupuncturist may diagnose this as an imbalance here between *Kidney, Liver* and *Heart*.

Alongside this spiritual, mental, emotional aspect of the *Heart* is a second more functional physical aspect. This is the *Heart Governor*, also referred to as the *Pericardium*, the sixth *Zang*. The Chinese name for it (*Xin Zhu*) may be translated as 'that through which the *Heart* commands'. Often the more physical problems of the *Heart*, such as palpitations or circulatory disorders, are treated via the *Pericardium* rather than the *Heart* itself, although there is some overlap.

The *Heart* relates to *Fire*, Summer, *Heat*, the colour red and the emotion of happiness. Symptoms of disharmony include: mental/emotional disturbances, insomnia, dizziness, palpitations, restlessness, irritability.

The Kidneys (*Shen*)

Traditionally the *Kidneys* govern the conservators of life. They represent that which pushes the organism to the actualization of its potential, sometimes called the evolutionary force within. The *Kidneys* are the Root of Life, they store *Jing* (see p.71), which is the basis of matter, the essence of life, and the basis for all growth, development, and sexuality. Storing and maintaining the quality of *Jing* is therefore the most important function of the *Kidneys*. They also govern the *Body Fluids* and nourish the bones and bone marrow. This relationship with the bone marrow involves them in the formation of *Blood*. In storing the *Jing*, the *Kidneys* also have an intimate relationship with the brain and spinal cord, and hence the nervous system.

The strength of the *Kidneys* determines the strength of the constitution. Their state can be assessed through the state of the teeth and hair. They are associated especially with the ears. Although basically a *Yin* organ, the *Kidneys* have both a *Yin* and a *Yang* aspect, known as *Kidney Fire* and *Kidney Water*.

Kidney Fire refers to the energetic aspect of the *Kidneys* – that which fuels the transformation of energies and substances. *Kidney Water* refers to the fluid, protecting, nourishing aspect of the *Kidneys*. *Kidney Fire* is sometimes called 'Ming Men', usually translated as 'The Gate of Destiny', which refers to the area between the *Kidneys* where the transformation of energies takes place. The acupuncture point *Ming Men*, located on the spine at the level of the waist, is used to increase basic energy levels and to tonify *Kidney Yang*.

The *Kidneys* are related to *Water*, Winter, coldness, the colour black and the emotion of fear. Signs of *Kidney* disharmony include: lack of energy, lower backache, dark circles under the eyes, dizziness, tinnitus (constant ringing in the ears), poor memory, impotence, night sweating.

The Lungs (*Fei*)

The *Lungs* are the rhythmic regulators of life. The cycle of energy throughout the body begins in the *Lungs*. The *Lungs* therefore govern the *Qi* and work with the *Heart* in maintaining the rhythm of pulmonary and cellular respiration.

Known as the roof of the Organs, the *Lungs* are responsible for making energy descend, and for distributing *Qi* to all parts of the body including the skin, the pores, and the

Kidneys A nurse in her 30s comes with sciatica. The pain is severe, starting in the left buttock and extending down the leg to the ankle. Casetaking reveals a lot of lifting of patients in her work and recently a state of exhaustion from extensive night duty. She has always tended to lower .backaches. Her doctor has prescribed painkillers and told her to rest. The acupuncturist diagnoses a weakness of the *Kidney* energy and treats with massage and moxibustion as well as needles. Relief is felt during treatment and in subsequent treatments the *Kidneys* are strengthened to prevent recurrence.

Spleen A woman comes with abnormal uterine bleeding. The bleeding is not excessive but slow and continuous, often several days before the period. Conventional tests have found no problems. Case-taking shows a history of miscarriage and a tendency to put on weight easily, with excessive use of dairy foods in the diet. These factors indicate a weakness in the *Spleen*. The patient is advised to reduce dairy foods, which can interfere with Spleen functioning, and by working mainly on *Spleen* and *Kidney* meridians the bleeding lessens over a period of months, finally disappearing completely.

body hair, with which the *Lungs* have a special relationship. The *Lungs* also help fluids to descend to the *Kidneys* and diffuse a fine vapour over the surface of the skin to moisten it. Many skin complaints are treated by strengthening the *Lungs*.

The openness of the *Lungs* to the outside, as well as their connection to the most peripheral and exterior parts of the body, make them particularly susceptible to outside attack. They govern the throat and nose, parts often affected in an acute attack on the *Lungs*, for instance in tonsillitis or the common cold.

The *Lungs* relate to *Metal*, Autumn dryness, the colour white, and the emotion of grief. Symptoms of disharmony include: coughing, tiredness, shortness of breath, white complexion, phlegm, skin problems, sadness and oppression.

The Spleen (*Pi*)

The Chinese concept of the *Spleen* is a much wider concept than the anatomical organ of Western medicine. Some sources – particularly those from Korea and Japan – include the *Pancreas* in the *Spleen* function.

The *Spleen* is the transformer and transporter. With the *Stomach* it transforms food and drink into subtle, assimilable essences, so helping to produce both *Blood* and *Qi*. It therefore effectively determines the efficient uptake of nourishment from food and sees that this is properly distributed to the Organs and body tissues. It is related to the mouth and its state can be assessed in the lips.

The *Spleen* influences the form of the body and the distribution of the flesh. Weight problems will often be diagnosed as being related to the *Spleen*. It also controls the ability to relate harmoniously to the environment, and to regulate the body's energies according to the energies of the outside world. An extension of this is the ability to assimilate the energy of the *Earth* in the form of food, and to distribute it evenly among the five *Zang*.

The *Spleen*, being at the centre, controls the *central Qi*. This energy is responsible for holding the abdominal organs in their correct place. Many cases of prolapse are regarded as being due to a weakness of the *Spleen*. It also 'contains' the *Blood*, preventing leakage from the blood vesels. Different types of haemorrhage can therefore be linked to the *Spleen*.

The *Spleen* relates to *Earth*, the centre, the colour yellow, and *Dampness*; mentally it is seen in the free flow of ideas. Over-concentration, obsession and unproductive thought suggest a *Spleen* imbalance. Symptoms of disharmony include: fatigue, wasting of flesh, obesity, digestive problems, diarrhoea with undigested food, bloated abdomen, prolapse, thoughts going round and round.

The Liver (*Gan*)

The *Liver* is a very active organ and governs the free flow of energy around the body – energy not only to move the muscles, respond and adapt to situations, but also to stimulate the mind and the emotions. Having the character of *Wood*, the *Liver* generates all movement – movement of *Qi*, movements of the body, discharge of bile to stimulate digestion or anything that 'moves' you emotionally.

Stagnation, whether physical, mental or emotional, comes under the realm of the *Liver*. It is seen as particularly sensitive to emotional changes. Frustration, irritability, stress at the lower end of the scale right up to anger, shouting, hysteria and violence at the top end – all indicate problems in the *Liver Qi*. It is also responsible for the storage and release of *Blood* around the body, although not in the same way as the *Heart*, which provides rhythm and regulation. When the body is at rest the *Blood* is stored in the *Liver*, and if the *Liver* is unable to store the *Blood* there may be restless sleep and dreaming. In activity the *Blood* is released to the muscles, giving nourishment and allowing movement once more.

The *Liver* motivates movement and ensures freedom from blockages. It is involved in most menstrual disorders. Many cases of premenstrual tension are due to stagnation of the *Liver Qi*, often causing depression and frustration.

The *Liver* meridian encircles the genitals, and the *Liver* may often be involved in sexual problems.

Called 'the Spring in the body', the *Liver* has a strong upward movement and tends to hyperactivity. This can rise very strongly causing violent symptoms such as explosive temper, splitting headaches, nosebleeds, and a bitter taste in the mouth.

Being responsible for movement, the *Liver* is implicated where this has either gone wild – for example in epilepsy, and convulsions – or stops completely – for example in paralysis after a stroke. Degenerative disorders such as Parkinsonism are also related to the *Liver*.

Liver A man of 42 comes with migraine headaches. The migraines are violent, coming from the back of the head and settling over the right eye, causing disturbed vision. They usually lead to a bitter taste in the mouth and often vomiting. The acupuncturist notes the high colour of the cheeks and discovers an increasing tendency to irritability both at home and at work. Surprisingly the patient still drinks spirits regularly every evening. The pulse is tight and wiry. The acupuncturist diagnoses an excess of *Liver Yang*, aggravated by the heating effect of the alcohol. The patient is advised to reduce alcohol intake substantially and treatment is directed to bringing down the *Fire* of the *Liver* with *Gallbladder* and *Liver* points while nourishing the *Yin* aspect of the *Liver* with *Kidney* points. The migraines substantially lessen in intensity and frequency, finally resolving completely.

The *Liver* governs the muscles and its state can be assessed from the nails. It is specially related to the eyes (often affected in *Liver*-type headaches).

The *Liver* corresponds to *Wood*, Spring, *Wind*, the colour green, growth and movement. Its related emotion is anger or frustration. Symptoms of disharmony include: depression, frustration, pains or distension in the sides, menstrual disorders, swollen and painful breasts, blurred vision, sudden, violent headaches, often one-sided.

Zang Organs

The *Zang* Organs are really ways of handling energy. The *Kidneys* are the foundation, giving strength and stability from below; the *Liver* expresses life, full of dynamic movement and power; the *Heart* is the quiet central point that governs all, and is responsible for radiance; the *Spleen* is the transformer constantly nourishing and maintaining; the *Lungs* are the rhythmic regulators that govern the breath of life. Each has its own sphere of action and when they interact correctly they maintain good health.

Fu Organs

The *Fu*, or hollow Organs, are considered to be less refined than *Zang* Organs. They deal with impure substances as the *Zang* deal with the pure. Their functions are similar to the Western concepts of the organs that carry the same names, and they play an important part in fluid metabolism.

They are the *Stomach, Small Intestine, Large Intestine, Bladder, Gallbladder* and the *Three Heater,* which has no analagous Western concept. A thumbnail sketch of each *Fu* organ will demonstrate their function in acupuncturists' terms.

The Stomach (*Wei*)

In Chinese terms, the functions of the *Stomach* include those of the oesophagus and duodenum as well. *Stomach* therefore implies the entire food pathway from the mouth to the *Small Intestine.* Its function is closely related to the *Spleen* – a *Yin/Yang* pair under the *Earth* Phase controlling nourishment. The *Stomach* is the source of the six *Fu* and the five *Zang*, 'the Sea of Liquids and Cereals'. It 'rots and ripens' the food, sending the impure down to the *Small Intestine* while the pure is sent upward by the *Spleen*. It is considered easily affected by alcohol or spicy food, leading to excessive *Heat* in the *Stomach*.

The Small Intestine (*Xiao Chang*)

Here the separation of pure and impure is continued, the pure going to the *Spleen*, the liquids being sent to the *Bladder*, and the solid waste to the *Large Intestine*. Linked with the *Heart* in the *Fire* Phase, the *Small Intestine* discriminates between what is needed and what is not.

The Large Intestine or Colon (*Da Chang*)

Responsible for the final transformation of food products into faeces and their evacuation, the *Large Intestine* is linked with the *Lungs* in the *Metal* Phase, responsible for contraction and downward movement.

The Bladder (*Pang Guang*)

Considered to collect fluids from *Lungs, Kidneys, Small Intestine* and *Large Intestine*, the *Bladder* transforms, retains and expels them as urine. Under the control of the *Kidneys* and the *Water* Phase, it is responsible for water balance in the body.

The Gallbladder (*Dan*)

Holding a special position in Chinese medicine, the *Gallbladder* not only discharges bile but is also responsible for the power to put things into action. It has a concentrated strength that provides the ability to make decisions and act. Closely linked with the *Liver* in the *Wood* Phase, it shares the characteristic of impetuous movement. Migraines – from stagnation of *Liver Qi* – often follow the path of the *Gallbladder* meridian up the back of the neck, across the back of the skull and over to the eyes.

The Three Heater (*San Jiao*)

Not an organ as such, the *Three Heater* is the ensemble of all the Organs functioning together on three levels in the trunk. The *Upper Heater* (or *Jiao*) – with the *Heart* and the *Lungs* – is compared to a mist. The *Lungs* acting on *Qi* and the *Heart's* link with *Shen* make this an area of refined energies. The *Middle Jiao* is a muddy pool – home of the *Stomach* and the *Spleen* – that transforms food and drink, making the clear ascend and the unclear descend. The *Lower Jiao* is a ditch where the impure and fluids are worked on by the *Intestines,* the *Bladder*, and the *Kidneys*. The *Triple Heater* ensures proper movement of *Qi* and fluids throughout the body. If it becomes disordered, swelling can result.

Stomach A patient comes with a burning sensation in the gastric region. He has been diagnosed as having a peptic ulcer and is on antacids which can temporarily relieve the pains, but have done nothing long term. Further questioning shows great thirst, bad breath, mouth ulcers and a tendency to constipation. The tongue is red with a thick, yellow coating. The pulse is rapid and slippery. The acupucturist diagnoses intense *Heat* in the *Stomach*. All heating foods – such as spices and alcohol – are withdrawn from the diet and clearing and cleansing foods substituted. Treatment is given mainly on *Yang Ming* meridians – *Stomach* and *Large Intestine* – to clear the *Heat*, cool the *Fire* and bring normal functioning back to the *Stomach*. The pains disappear on their own as normality is restored.

All the Organs – especially the *Zang*, are responsible for 'handling' the *Shen, Qi, Jing, Blood* and *Body Fluids*. But how does *Qi* circulate – not just within the Three Heater in the trunk, but also to the head and to the muscles of the arms and legs that allow us to move and act?

This brings us to the pathways of energy – better known as channels or meridians – which run through us all and which the acupuncturist uses to stimulate, disperse or redirect the *Qi*.

The meridian system (*Jing-Luo*)

Different places have different qualities. The frenetic tension and excitement of New York, the clean-cut freshness of the Alps, the dusty poverty of backstreet Delhi, or the fresh seaside air of the Cornish cliffs, all have clearly identifiable qualities. To live in a valley is different to living in a wood, by a stream, in a city; the top of a hill is different to the bottom, by nature of its position. All of these things we know and feel – they are obvious and often form the unconscious basis for our choice of where we live, or where we go on holiday.

The Chinese would say each of those different places has a certain quality of *Qi* – and they would be talking of more than just fresh air. The study of *Qi* in the landscape is called *Feng-Shui* (literally *Wind-Water*) and has been used for centuries to determine the best places to build houses for the living as well as temples and tombs for the dead. Acupuncture is the *Feng-Shui* of the body.

The Chinese word *Jing* (a different word to *Jing* – meaning essence) is weakly translated as meridian or channel. An analysis of its written character gives the idea of a flux or a flow – fine, imperceptible, threadlike streams which at a deep level nourish and organize the body. Just as a dowser is sensitive to streams or currents in the earth so an acupuncturist must have a similar sensitivity to the invisible currents in the body in order to find the 'points'.

The points are places that give access to these energy streams. In fact they are not so much points as hollows or holes. In scientific language, they are places of lowered resistance and higher conductance. In the future, it is probable that each of the points will be shown to have a particular frequency, so explaining its effects on the body as a whole and on its related organ in particular.

The *Jing-Luo* system is a complex network with different

Different places have different energy levels and can be beautiful and stimulating in their own way. The quintessential urban skyline of New York has a different atmosphere to a peaceful alpine scene. The Chinese regard these different essences of place as different qualities of Qi, the same energy that courses through our bodies.

levels, ranging from muscle meridians that cover the surface of the body to the Eight Extraordinary Meridians that act as reservoirs at a deep level. Its function is to circulate the *Qi* and *Blood* throughout the body, protecting and nourishing, and ensuring communication between interior and exterior, top and bottom.

The balance and harmonious flow of this energy can be influenced by the insertion of fine needles into the acupuncture points, dispersing where there is excess, tonifying in deficiency, cooling in *Heat*, warming in *Cold*, moving in stagnation, calming in agitation. It is a subtle but immensely practical system that does nothing but open gates so that harmony can restore itself on its own.

The main meridians are all connected with the Organs and are the means of spreading the influence of each Organ over the body. Running vertically up the midline of the body are the two 'primary' meridians, *Du Mai* – 'Governor vessel' – uniting all the *Yang* on the back, and *Ren Mai* – 'Conception vessel' – uniting all the *Yin* on the front. There are twelve main meridians, six *Yin* and six *Yang*, and each relates to one of the *Zang-Fu*.

The *Qi* flows in a continual cycle round the twelve meridians. Starting in the chest, it flows down the inside of the arm to the hand, changing at the fingers to the outside of the hand and moving up the outside of the arm to the head. From the head it flows down the body, down the outside of the legs to the feet and toes from where it ascends up the inside of the leg, up the trunk to the chest again.

Even from such a basic view of the meridians, simple conclusions can be drawn. For example, needles may be inserted into a *Yang* meridian of the foot to remove excess energy from the head or into a *Yin* meridian of the foot to increase the energy of the abdominal organs.

MERIDIANS RELATED TO THE SIX DIVISIONS OF YIN AND YANG

Small Intestine	}	TAI YANG	Lung	}	TAI YIN
Bladder		(Greater Yang)	Spleen		(Greater Yin)
Three Heater	}	SHAO YANG	Heart Governor	}	JUE YIN
Gall Bladder		(Lesser Yang)	Liver		(Extreme Yin)
Colon	}	YANG MING	Heart	}	SHAO YIN
Stomach		(Bright Yang)	Kidney		(Lesser Yin)

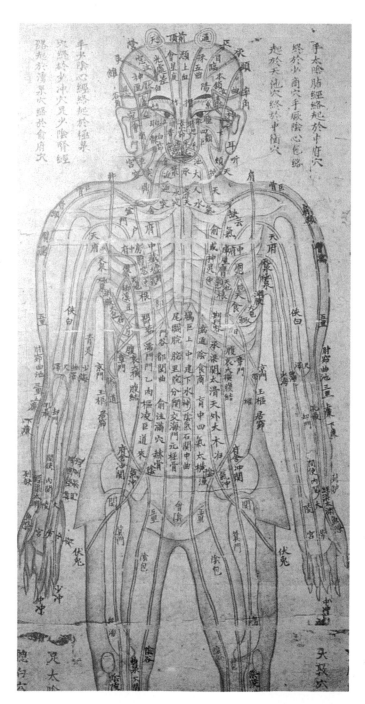

Through the centuries many representations have been made of the meridian system and the location of acupuncture points. Here a picture from the Ming dynasty indicates the meridians and names of points.

Causes of disease

The Chinese classify the causes of disease under several categories: congenital, poisons, parasites, accidents, excessive sexual activity, improper diet, exercise and general lifestyle. Two other major factors are the emotions internally and the climates externally. A brief study of these will give further insight into the Chinese medical perspective.

Internal causes of disease

The study of the effects of emotions can be traced right back to the earliest texts on Chinese medicine over 2000 years ago. Each of the Five Phases has a corresponding emotional tendency (see p.62-3). As orthodox medicine is now beginning to realize, emotions can profoundly effect physical health.

Fire – joy – upward movement

Fire The patient feels restless, depressed and bored, with dramatic mood swings. He has a history of dependence on stimulant drugs and alcohol but no longer takes drugs of any kind. The acupuncturist diagnoses a case of 'disturbed *Shen*' brought about by excessive stimulation and seeking after excitement. Points are chosen on the *Heart* meridian to calm the *Shen* and 'empty' the *Heart*. Points on the *Kidney* meridian are also used to help the will and to give the necessary emotional grounding.

Fire has an upward movement which corresponds to the emotion of joy or happiness. Although we may immediately feel that joy must be positive and find it difficult to imagine a state of too much joy, the Chinese believe that joy, as all the other emotions, must be kept in balance. Often the Western concept of joy requires excitement and stimulation, rather than a feeling of inner contentment and peace. This is considered to be a 'false joy' and may be damaging to the *Heart*.

Too much joy or excitement will cause the energy to rise and scatter, and may produce a condition known as 'floating *Shen*' or Spirit, or 'the Spirit not housed'.

The upward movement of *Fire* requires the balancing effect of *Water* with its downward energy. *Fire/Water* imbalance is one of the most common disharmonies encountered by the acupuncturist, especially in emotional problems. As in nature, *Fire* and *Water* exist in a state of mutual control and balance, and so must this delicate balance and control be maintained within the individual.

The *Kidneys*, with their cooling effect and downward movement, govern the will and intention. It is this bringing of thought into action, and potential into reality, which acts as a balance to *Shen*. It gives root to ideas and allows them to grow and flourish. Without this, the *Shen* would be unanchored, a state which may ultimately lead to instability and even madness. The *Kidneys* provide the necessary grounding in reality.

Traditional acupuncture exhibits a detailed understanding of the various kinds of depression and psychic disturbances related to the imbalance of *Fire* and *Water*, and treatment can be very effective.

Water – fear – downward movement

Fear is considered to affect primarily the *Kidneys*, making the energy descend and thereby losing control of the two lower orifices – incontinence and diarrhoea are well known both to soldiers before a battle and students before exams!

Fear is extremely draining and depleting in the long term, and fear of facing life is at the root of many cases of depression and phobias. This is a two-way process. Weakened *Kidney* energy can lead to a fearful attitude to life, or the inability to put ideas into action.

Wood – anger – outward movement

Wood has an outward, expansive movement, and its associated emotion is anger. The corresponding human sound is shouting.

Just as joy is not always positive, so anger is not always negative, and each of the emotions has its rightful place in the human psyche. It is only when one emotion is overindulged and overcomes the others that it may be considered harmful.

Anger makes the energy move outward and upward, but suppressed anger, which may be called frustration, blocks energy and causes stagnation. The *Liver* function is the most susceptible to this stagnation, which can in turn lead to anger and irritability.

Metal – sadness – contracting movement

Metal has the opposite movement to *Wood*, of contraction, withdrawing into the interior. Sadness is seen to cause the same movement within the body, often resulting in a feeling of oppression in the chest and consequent rounding of the shoulders: precisely the posture so often seen in someone who is sad and depressed.

This pressure on the chest brought about by a hunched, shrunken, round-shouldered posture affects the breathing patterns, and the *Lungs* are no longer able to expand to their full capacity and take sufficient energy from the air. This in turn will affect the quality of *Qi* throughout the whole body.

Wood Woman in her early 40s complains of severe pre-menstrual tension and painful, scanty periods. Her two children are now at college and she is restless and frustrated, feeling that she has missed out on life. Treatment aims to remove stagnation and 'stuckness' in the *Liver* channel and to harmonize the *Liver* and *Gallbladder*. *Wood* represents movement, growth and expansion; and lack of movement, whether physical, mental or emotional will affect the *Liver* function. Strengthening the *Liver* and *Gallbladder* function will help to relieve the stagnation in the channels causing the menstrual problems, and to release the anger and frustration giving a more clear feeling of direction in life.

Deep breathing exercises, and concentration on posture, will genuinely help to alleviate long-term grief and sadness. It is sometimes difficult for us to grasp that merely physical methods can help an emotional or mental problem, but this is only because our culture has taught us to see the mind and the body as separate entities.

In Chinese medicine there is no such separation. Anything that happens in the body will ultimately affect the mind and vice versa.

Earth – thinking – centred movement

The *Earth* is the centre, and governs thought. In its negative state it may be expressed in muddled thinking which has no direction, such as obsession or constant worrying. The effect of this is that the *Qi* becomes knotted and stuck. This can disturb the transforming function of the *Spleen*, leading to abdominal symptoms such as poor digestion, stomach ulcers, anorexia, loss of appetite, and heaviness in body and mind.

But in its positive aspect the *Spleen* represents intelligent thought, and in its central position unites the spiritual aspiration of the *Heart* with the basic grounding and 'know-how' of the *Kidneys*.

Communication also belongs in the realm of the *Spleen* – the ability to externalize thought and promote the exchange of ideas, which supports the idea of the *Spleen* providing communication with the environment.

Emotions cause motion and the Chinese – with their emphasis on the observation of movement – made detailed studies of them as internal causes of disease. The relevance of this to modern men and women, in view of the turmoil of many people's lives, is unquestionable.

External causes of disease

Just as each of the emotions was assessed as a particular movement or vibration that resonates in a particular way, affecting especially the related organ, so it is with the 'climates', *Wind, Cold, Heat, Dampness* and *Dryness*. Each of them has a particular quality and therefore a particular effect.

They are used in Chinese medicine in two ways – firstly as the effect of actual external environmental conditions; and secondly the climates are used to describe the pattern of working in internal conditions.

Earth Patient is unable to sleep. She cannot stop thinking about the problems of the day and the same thoughts go round and round in the head. When she does sleep, she has recurring dreams of trival everyday matters. She feels tired and listless and wants to lie down. The treatment aims to strengthen the *Spleen* which governs thinking, and to harmonize the *Earth* and *Fire*, giving direction and spiritual content to the thought.

Spring is the season of growth and burgeoning energy. It exemplifies the change from Yin *to* Yang, *pushing what is inside outside with the forceful impetuosity of the* Wood *Phase. Its climate is* Wind *— fast, changeable and penetrating.*

Wind (Feng)

Associated with Spring and the *Wood* Phase, *Wind* is considered to be the spearhead of disease because of its penetrating quality. *Wind* is fast, sudden and changeable. It combines easily with other climates — *Wind-Cold* and *Wind-Heat* for example — giving them the edge to penetrate the body's defences. Acute illnesses of sudden onset affecting the top of the body — the head and neck for example, such as influenza, coughs, and colds — are seen in Chinese terms as *Wind* attacking the *Lungs*, the organ most open to the exterior.

Specific points to 'expel the *Wind*' are used in such cases. At the same time, the defending *Qi* must have been weak to allow penetration and this is also strengthened to prevent recurrence.

External *Wind* is a relatively superficial phenomenon compared to Internal *Wind*, however. Here a situation arises where the *Yin* and *Yang* of the body grow dangerously out of balance, allowing *Wind* to develop. This affects especially the *Liver* and very severe symptoms develop, such as blurred vision, vertigo, violent headaches, uncontrolled movements of the limbs, and difficulty speaking or walk-

Wind A man comes at the onset of a cold. He has itching in the throat, a runny nose, a slight cough with clear, white catarrh, feels chilly and is better from warmth. The acupuncturist diagnoses *Wind-Cold* invading the *Lungs* and uses moxa and needles to strengthen the *Lungs* and expel the *Wind*. The 'cold' resolves within a day or two preventing complications or the need for medication.

ing. (The word 'typhoon' – associated with sudden havoc and immense damage – comes from the Chinese *Tai Feng*, meaning Great Wind.) If this reaches an extreme there are all the symptoms of a stroke – sudden unconsciousness, inability to speak, deviation of mouth and eye, partial paralysis.

This is just one type of *Liver Wind*; others produce problems such as epilepsy, convulsions, or long-term tics and tremors. The treatment for example of stroke patients using a combination of acupuncture and remedial exercise has a good prognosis. The earlier that treatment is started, however, the better the results are likely to be.

Mists, mellow fruitfulness and a certain sadness charcterizes the Western notion of Autumn. In Chinese philosophy it is also linked with sadness, a time of withdrawal and contraction as Yang *turns to* Yin, *the* Metal Phase *where the leaves dry up and fall and the fruits are set containing the seeds for the coming year.*

Cold, Heat, Dampness and *Dryness* are seen in a similar way to *Wind*. For instance, certain points are described as expelling *Cold*, or cooling *Heat*.

Cold (Han)

Associated with Winter and the *Water* Phase, *Cold* slows, obstructs, blocks and hardens, causing contraction and severe, sharp, biting pains. The body becomes cold and underactive, and secretions (urine, stool, phlegm, for instance) become watery, clear and copious.

Heat (Re)

Associated with Summer and the *Fire* Phase, *Heat* warms, activates, and moves to produce redness, inflammation and fever. It causes reckless movement, injures the *Blood* and damages *Body Fluids*. People become restless and irritable; secretions become thick, hot and yellow. An acupuncturist will often ask about the nature of a patient's phlegm, and look at the coating on their tongue in order to differentiate between *Cold* and *Heat*.

Dampness (Shi)

Associated with the *Earth* Phase, *Dampness* lingers, stagnates and obstructs. It is slow and draining. *Dampness* generates a heavy, stiff, aching, dull feeling. It clogs things up so that secretions are thick, sticky and copious – typical examples are yellow discharges from the eyes, cloudy urine, heavy vaginal discharges, and skin conditions with pus that oozes. *Dampness* is hard to shift. A thick, greasy tongue coating indicates *Dampness*. Lumps and tumours are often considered as an accumulation of *Dampness*.

Dryness (Zao)

Associated with Autumn and the *Metal* Element, *Dryness* is dehydration, an absence of the fluids that lubricate and moisten internally and externally. It is a drying out of the *Yin* that is so vital to life and can be seen in dry skin, mouth, lips, nails, and hair externally, as well as insufficient internal secretions, indicated by thirst, constipation, or scanty urine.

Weaving the pattern

This brief outline of the principles of Chinese medicine indicates how acupuncture approaches what the West calls 'disease'. The fact that, for example, you have asthma is not

4 types of arthritis In Chinese medicine arthritis is seen broadly as *'Bi'* meaning Obstruction or Blockage and the way that blockage manifests determines how it is treated.

● **Wind Bi** The pain in the joints is widespread and moves from one area of the body to another. There is often accompanying fever and chills, a rapid pulse and yellow coating to the tongue.

● **Damp Bi** The joints are swollen, stiff and aching, aggravated by contact with water and wet weather. There is a general feeling of heaviness and a greasy coating to the tongue.

● **Cold Bi** The joints are cold to the touch and are definitely improved with heat. The pains are severe, sharp and biting. The tongue coating is thin and white, the pulse wiry and tight.

● **Heat Bi** The joints are red, hot, swollen and sensitive to the touch. The mouth is dry, the urine dark. The tongue coating is yellow, the pulse rapid.

Individual cases can be combinations of the above. In all, the background cause of the Obstruction must be rectified.

very significant; how that asthma manifests itself in you and how those symptoms are related to your health in general, your constitution, your personality, and so on is what interests your acupuncturist.

An acupuncturist assesses the whole picture – the interplay of the *Zang-Fu* Organs, the balance of the Five Elements, the balance of *Blood* and *Qi*, of *Yin* and *Yang*. This is a bewildering mass of interconnecting information. To organise it into cogent useful data, acupuncturists use a classification system called the Eight Principal Patterns.

The Eight Principle Patterns (*Ba Gang*)

The Eight Principle Patterns guide the acupuncturist through a maze of signs and symptoms towards an accurate diagnosis tailored to the individual concerned. They are represented as further differentiations of *Yin/Yang*:

YIN	YANG
Interior	Exterior
Deficiency	Excess
Cold	Heat

Interior/Exterior

This pattern relates to the depth of the disorder, both in terms of location in the body and in terms of severity.

Exterior conditions generally arise from an attack by one of the external climates – *Wind, Cold, Heat, Dryness,* or *Dampness* (see p.87-9). They come on suddenly, last only a short while and affect the superficial parts of the body, giving rise to chills, fever, headaches or body aches.

Interior conditions generally arise from internal causes such as diet, or emotions. They come on gradually and are chronic, long-term disorders affecting organs, deep tissues, or bones. Symptoms are relatively deep-seated, and include changes in appetite or bowel movements, internal discomfort or pain. They are reflected in changes in the tongue.

Deficiency/Excess

This pattern establishes the strength of the body's resistance, and provides an assessment of its vitality and ability to withstand disease.

Deficiency shows an emptiness generally and reflects an insufficiency of *Blood, Qi* or *Body Fluids* or the underactivity of a particular Organ. General signs are frailness, weakness, tiredness, inactivity and weak voice. There may be shallow breathing, with pains relieved by pressure. The pulse is weak, the tongue pale.

Excess shows either a strong reaction to an external attack or a picture of accumulation and stagnation. General signs are of heavy, forceful movement, heavy breathing, congestion, fullness, bloating with pains worse for pressure. The pulse is strong and full.

Cold/Heat
This pattern helps to understand the nature of the disorder. If the body is attacked by external *Heat* or if the *Yin* of the body is depleted, there will be signs of *Heat*. Conversely, if the body is attacked by *Cold* or the *Yang* of the body is depleted, there will be *Cold*.

Signs of *Cold* show in a pale complexion, slow movements, withdrawn manner, wanting to curl up, a general feeling of chill, lack of thirst or wanting only warm drinks. Pains are better for warmth. There may be diarrhoea and profuse pale urine. The pulse is slow. The tongue is pale and swollen, with white fur.

Heat shows in a red face, and is typified by fever and a dislike of warmth. Irritability, thirst, constipation are also signs, as are scanty dark urine and red skin eruptions. The pulse is fast. The tongue is red, with yellow fur.

Using the Eight Principle Patterns
These categories allow refinement of diagnosis, clarifying and further differentiating the pattern, so that it can be seen, for example, not only that the *Liver* is affected, but also that the *Liver Blood* is deficient where there is numbness, spasm, trembling with scanty periods and blurred vision; or that the *Liver Qi* is stagnant where there are pains at the sides, sighing, swollen breasts and irritability; or that the *Liver Yang* is rising where the head is affected with dizziness, headache, insomnia and bad temper.

The detail becomes intricate and specific to the person being diagnosed. The theory and framework of the principles on which Chinese medicine rests come to life in each particular patient. Acupuncture itself is just the method of treatment.

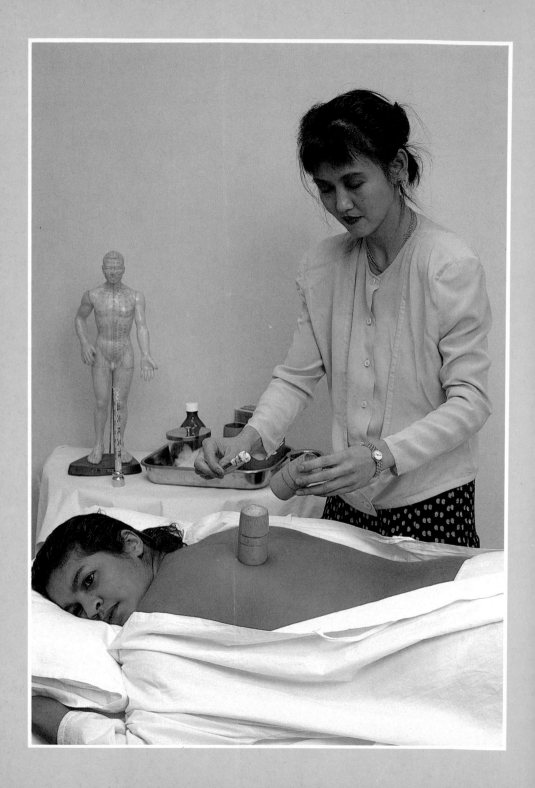

5

ACUPUNCTURE
IN ACTION

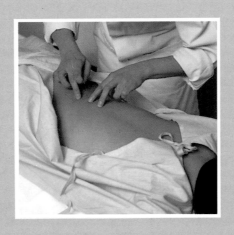

The link between the theory of Chinese medicine and the actual treatment of a patient is the process of diagnosis. To an acupuncturist, this is not simply a question of diagnosing a specific disease in the sense that Western doctors diagnose illness, but diagnosis of a pattern of disharmony peculiar to the individual patient.

In acupuncture as we have seen, diseases are rarely named as they are in the West. On a first visit to an acupuncturist, the patient may be surprised that the Western medical name for his or her problem is of little importance in forming a diagnosis. In fact, two patients with an identically named disease may be treated in a different way according to their particular pattern of symptoms and energetic imbalances. The practitioner examines all the patient's signs and symptoms in order to form a picture, but this picture may change and a patient is continually reassessed at each consultation.

The first visit is generally the longest, lasting about one hour, because the practitioner needs to spend more time making an initial diagnosis. As soon as the patient walks through the door, the diagnosis begins.

Diagnosis

The practitioner notes the way the patient walks and sits, and observes his or her facial expressions and so on before beginning to ask questions. In fact, questioning is only a part of the traditional Chinese method of acupuncture, and was sometimes considered to be the least important. The examination is actually divided into four stages: looking; listening and smelling; asking; and touching.

Looking This part of the diagnosis begins as soon as the patient enters the consultation room. It is most important to the acupuncturist to assess the 'spirit' of the patient, and this may be shown by the way he or she walks and moves, in the general bearing, facial expressions and responses. If the patient shows 'good spirit', it usually indicates that the condition is not serious. But it is also possible to have too much spirit – to move in an exaggerated way, to talk too much and in an excited manner – which may indicate an imbalance and suggest a *Yang*, or *Excess* state. If this state is accompanied by other signs of weakness, it suggests a state of False *Yang*, which implies that the deeper *Yin* aspects of the body are depleted to such an extent that they can no longer control the *Yang*.

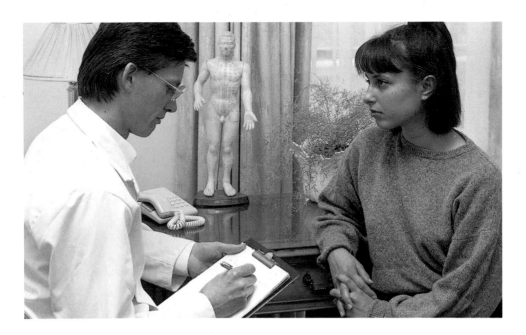

If the patient's face is pale, the skin lacks lustre, there is no shine to the eyes, and movements and responses are slow, the spirit (*Shen*) is weak, and there is a condition of *Deficiency*.

The patient's face is studied carefully for abnormal colouring. All the acupuncture meridians flow to the face, by their primary or secondary pathways, and the state of *Blood* and *Qi* is very evident. A red face may indicate *Heat*, whereas a white, withered face denotes a lack of *Blood*. Specific colours in certain areas of the face may relate to particular *Organ* problems (for example, black circles under the eyes indicate *Kidney* weakness). Red colouring relates to *Heat, Fire*, and possibly the *Heart*, whereas black or blue-black colouring relates to the *Kidneys*. It follows that a yellow face may indicate *Spleen* problems and/or *Dampness*; blue-green may indicate *Wind* or *Liver* involvement, and particularly stagnation, in which the liver is failing to provide movement. A white face may imply a lack of *Qi*, or a *Lung* problem.

The skin of the rest of the body may also be examined for colour, flesh tone, distribution of fat, appearance of body hair, and so on. Each practitioner tends to develop his or her own style of visual diagnosis within the tradition.

Acupuncturists will take a long time over a detailed case history at the first consultation. Without being intrusive, the practitioner may ask many questions that seem irrelevant to the patient but are essential to the diagnosis.

The tongue is a very important source of information for the acupuncturist. The shape, colour, coating and texture of the various parts of the tongue yield information about the state of the Organs.

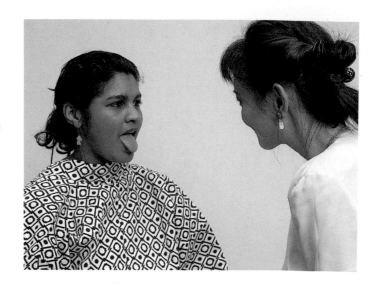

Observation of the tongue is possibly the most developed form of the 'looking' aspect of diagnosis. The tongue is studied for its general shape and colour, and the presence or lack of fur. Particular areas of the tongue are traditionally related to specific Organs. A healthy tongue should be reddish in colour with little or no fur. It should not appear swollen or contracted, neither should it have cracks on the surface or teeth marks along the sides.

TONGUE

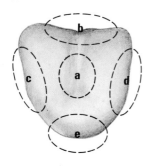

a *stomach*
b *kidneys*
c *liver* and *gallbladder*
d *liver* and *gallbladder*
e *lung/heart*

Tongue diagnosis Whole volumes have been written on tongue diagnosis, and here it is only possible to give an indication of what the practitioner is looking for.

Generally speaking, a red tongue indicates a *Yang* condition; a pale tongue, *Yin*. White fur may indicate *Cold*; thick, yellow fur, *Heat*. Red spots on the surface suggest heat, whereas dark purplish spots on the sides of the tongue show stagnation of *Blood*, which may often be seen in menstrual problems. Cracks in the tongue show *Heat, Dryness*, deficient *Yin* and therefore lack of *Fluids*, whereas a swollen tongue – often with tooth marks at the sides – shows a *Deficiency of Qi* and possibly *Dampness*.

It is important not to eat or drink anything that will discolour the tongue before the consultation. Coffee, fruit drinks and sweets all tend to discolour the fur and sometimes the body of the tongue, which can give a misleading picture.

Listening and smelling Most important in this aspect of diagnosis are the sound of the voice and the breathing. A loud assertive voice suggests a *Yang* pattern, and a weak timid voice suggests a *Yin* pattern. In the same way, coarse heavy breathing indicates excess whereas shallow breathing indicates a *Deficiency*. Coughing may be loud and sudden or in violent fits; or it may be weak and persistent.

The 'Human Sounds' category in the table of correspondences shows that each of the Five Phases has its own particular sound, and these sounds may help the practitioner to form a more precise diagnosis. A shouting voice suggests an angry temperament and possibly indicates a *Liver* or *Gallbladder* imbalance, whereas a weeping voice shows sadness and possibly *Lung* disharmony.

'Smelling' is rarely discussed in the West, because most people regard body smells as an embarrassing subject, and for this reason the art has been rather neglected by Western acupuncturists. Traditionally, however, the smells of the body and its excretions are important aids to diagnosis.

In modern China, two distinct smells are considered to distinguish a hot, excess condition from a cold, deficient one. The first smell is rotten and rancid, whereas the second is pungent and fishy. As with the sounds, some practitioners may use the smells listed under the Five Phases correspondences to identify particular Organ or function disharmonies.

Asking During the first consultation, a considerable amount of time is spent asking the patient details about his or her general condition. Questions can relate to all physical, emotional and energetic signs and symptoms. Although some of these may seem unrelated, all can help the acupuncturist to form a more complete picture of the patient's condition.

A full medical history is also taken, including details of past illnesses, operations and traumas, both mental and physical. Although it may not seem relevant to the patient, an emotional upset or a bereavement before the onset of a particular problem may provide the most important clue to understanding a particular pattern of disharmony. Similarly, an operation – although seemingly unrelated – may have affected the present complaint by interrupting the flow of energy along the meridian pathways. In addition, family traits and tendencies, and even the health of the patient's

The toes can play an important role in the acupuncturist's diagnosis. Three Yin *meridians begin at the toes; three* Yang *meridians end at the toes. Examination of the feet may indicate imbalances within the meridians. For example, the big toe sloping towards the second toe may indicate a weakness in the* Spleen *meridian.*

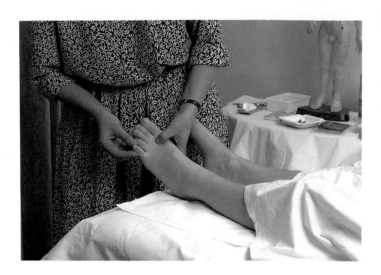

mother during pregnancy, provide significant information.

Other important questions to be answered concern sensations of heat and cold; perspiration, and whether this occurs during the day or at night; headaches, when they occur, and in what part of the head; urination and defaecation, including frequency of bladder movements, and any tendencies to constipation or diarrhoea. Women are asked about their menstrual cycle, in particular the length of the cycle, duration and heaviness of bleeding, and the existence of pain and discomfort. Diet and sleep patterns are also relevant.

Specific questions about the nature of any pain or discomfort, such as reactions to heat or cold, and to touch, all point to patterns of *Excess* and *Deficiency,* to imbalances of *Yin* and *Yang*.

If the pain is relieved by heat, a *Cold* condition is implied. If it is relieved by cold, there is a *Hot, Excess* condition. If the pain is better for massage or pressure, the condition is one of *Deficiency*. If it is made worse by pressure, the condition is of *Excess*. Pain that moves around the body is associated with *Wind*, and pain associated with heaviness and swelling implies *Damp*.

The sites of pains are also noted, even if they seem unrelated to the main complaint, because they may indicate blockages in the channels, or meridian pathways. For example, pain or weakness in the knees may point to a *Kidney* weakness, and pains in the genital area may point to a blockage in the *Liver* meridian.

For these reasons, it is most important to tell the acupuncturist about all your signs and symptoms, however irrelevant they may seem. Your failing memory may have apparently little connection to your lower back pain, but to the acupuncturist it may be your most telling symptom.

Touching The last of the four examinations is touching, also called palpation, and involves touching local areas of the body which may be painful, to feel for heat, cold, swelling, tightness or lack of skin tone. Specific acupuncture points may be touched to see if they are painful, particularly points on the abdomen and each side of the spine. These points have a particular relationship to the internal Organs, and pain under pressure would suggest imbalance. Some acupuncturists, particularly those trained in Japan, use the abdomen as one of the main areas of diagnosis.

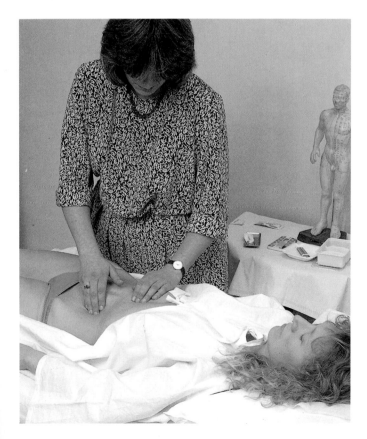

The Abdomen *contains the* Hara *and is a vital energy centre. Abdominal palpation can be used to ascertain the strength of this vital energy. Different areas of the abdomen also reflect the energy level in each Organ.*

The pulse In the category of touching, taking the pulse at the radial artery in the wrist is considered to be most important, and is often considered to be the acupuncturist's main diagnostic tool.

The pulse is taken at both wrists and in three positions, by the index, middle and ring finger.

The index finger is placed closest to the wrist, and the middle finger placed level with the bony protuberance of the radius bone on the outside of the wrist. Care must be taken to place the fingers correctly, and in proportion to the patient's body. A child's pulse, for example, is much closer together than an adult's, and that of a small-framed adult differs from the pulse of a larger, fatter adult.

The three pulse positions correspond to the Upper, Middle and Lower areas of the body (the Three *Jiao*, or *Three Heaters*), although over the centuries slightly different pulse pictures have evolved. The most basic pulse pictures are:

LEFT	RIGHT	LEFT	RIGHT
Heart	Lung	Fire	Metal
Liver	Spleen	Wood	Earth
Kidney/Yin	Kidney/Yang	Water	Fire

It is important that the patient (and, in fact, the practitioner) is relaxed before the pulse is taken, so if the patient has been hurrying to be on time for the appointment, he or she is often asked to lie quietly for a few minutes to enable the pulse to return to normal. The pulse is also affected if the patient is particularly nervous, and this must also be taken into consideration.

Traditionally, there are 28 pulse qualities, and the practitioner has to keep all of these in mind as he or she takes the pulse. The qualities are descriptions of the way the pulse feels to the fingertip, and include such categories as deep or superficial, full or empty, tight or wiry, slippery or choppy.

A healthy pulse is felt easily with only slight pressure, and does not fade with stronger pressure. It should fill all three positions on the wrists, and have an even, rhythmic flow. If a pulse appears to jump up from the surface of the skin, it is considered to be superficial, whereas if it is felt only with strong pressure, it is deep.

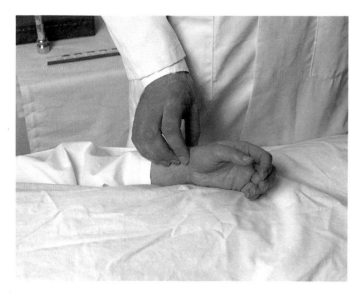

Taking the pulses has been one of the fundamental diagnostic methods of traditional Chinese medicine for the last 2,000 years, and is far more intricate than pulse taking in the West. It allows the practitioner to assess the balance of energy in the patient from three positions at the wrist. The depth, speed, general quality and overall balance of the pulses give the key to a patient's internal state.

The average speed of the pulse is 70-72 beats per minute, or 4 beats to each inhalation and exhalation, although children have a faster pulse, and athletes, for example, a slower one. A slippery pulse, said to feel like rolling a pearl in a basin, is very fluid and full, whereas a choppy pulse has no strength and feels irregular. A full pulse is large and rounded and can be felt at all levels, and an empty pulse may be indiscernible, or felt only slightly at the superficial level while disappearing under pressure.

The qualities can be divided into those relating to *Yin* and those relating to *Yang*:

YIN	YANG
slow	fast
deep	superficial
choppy	slippery
empty	full

Generally speaking, the *Yang* pulses indicate *Excess* and the *Yin* pulses *Deficiency*, but in practice each pulse shows a combination of types and the different pulse positions may present a different quality.

More than any other method of diagnosis, pulse-taking

requires skill and practice, and a particular sensitivity and concentration. The practitioner must first be able to feel the overall quality of the pulse, then to differentiate imbalances within the *Three Heaters* and, finally, the Organs. For instance, some pulse pictures show the *Yang* Organs in the position superficial to the related *Yin* Organs. All these different patterns must be woven together to form a picture of the patient's energy imbalances.

The tongue and the pulse The most important of the acupuncturist's diagnostic tools are observation of the tongue and feeling the pulse. These are traditionally called the 'two pillars' of the Four Examinations. Any acupuncturist who does not take time to look at the tongue and to feel the pulse has probably not received a traditional oriental training. Some schools tend to stress one system over another, and in others, colours of the face and body or observation of body odours may take the place of tongue diagnosis. However one sign of a well-trained acupuncturist is the attention he pays to these two aspects of diagnosis.

Treatment and techniques

After collecting together all the relevant information, the acupuncturist must formulate the treatment. This involves the choice of specific acupuncture points and possibly the use of moxibustion and massage. Some acupuncturists also prescribe herbs, although Chinese herbs are still relatively unknown in the West. Traditionally, acupuncture forms part of an overall treatment system that includes the use of herbs, massage, diet and exercise.

Zhen and Jiu The Chinese term usually translated as acupuncture is made up of two characters, *Zhen* and *Jiu*. *Zhen* represents piercing metal, and refers to the needles. *Jiu* represents 'slow heating' and refers to the application of a burning herb called moxa or common mugwort (*Artemisia vulgaris*), in a technique known as moxibustion.

The insertion of fine needles into acupuncture points and the application of heat through moxibustion are the most common methods of treatment used by acupuncturists, although they may also use massage in conjunction with needles or, in some cases – if the patient is particularly afraid of needles for instance – they may use massage or pressure on the acupuncture points without using needles at all.

Acupuncture needles The needles used in acupuncture are extremely fine and are usually made of stainless steel, although some practitioners prefer to use needles made of silver and gold for their respective sedation and tonification properties. Most practitioners will use disposable needles if requested, although all registered acupuncturists are required to carry out stringent sterilization procedures so this is not strictly necessary.

The needles should not cause pain when they are inserted. Nevertheless there is a 'needle sensation', which may be described as a tingling, or a feeling of numbness radiating from the needle. This sensation tends to differ from patient to patient and also depends upon the particular points chosen. Sometimes there is also a distinct twinge as the needle comes into contact with the *Qi*, but this is only momentary. The points in the forearm and the lower leg are the most frequently used, and these points give more feeling of needle sensation than those on, for example, the chest or head. Occasionally, the limb may feel heavy and numb, but this is a natural reaction and should not give the patient any cause for concern.

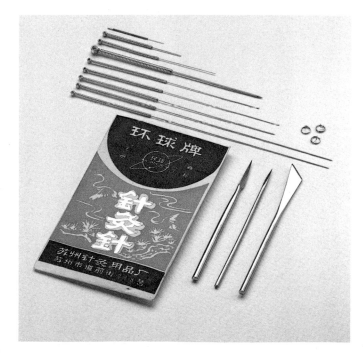

The tools of the trade: various sizes of acupuncture needles, ring needles and, to the right of the packet, pricking tools.

The standard needles are used to stimulate the meridians at the acupuncture points, only the smaller sizes being in common use. The ring needles are placed over an acupuncture point and then covered with a plaster to hold them in place for a day or two to provide continual low-level stimulation.

The pricking tools are rarely used except in instances of high fever.

Two needles have been inserted at Bladder point 23 to stimulate the Kidneys. *The acupuncturist feels carefully along the spine to locate the next point.*

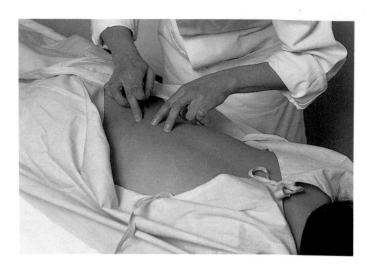

Does acupuncture hurt? The question 'does it hurt?' is probably the most frequently asked by people who are thinking of seeking treatment from an acupuncturist for the first time. It is a simple question, but it is difficult to answer. On the one hand, some patients show very little sensitivity to the needles, and do not feel anything when they are inserted. On the other hand, there may be increased sensitivity in particular areas or on particular meridians, relating to an energy imbalance. Furthermore a patient may feel more sensitive to the needles on one occasion than on another. In general, however, treatment should not be painful, and when needle sensation occurs it should not last more than a few seconds.

In modern China it is the general practice to use thicker needles, and to apply 'needle manipulation' to achieve a required response. Some western practitioners tend to use this approach, and there will possibly be more pain. On the other hand, Japanese practitioners use hairlike needles with a cylindrical guiding rod, which tends to reduce the pain of needle insertion to the minimum. Most acupuncturists tend to find their own style of effective needle technique somewhere between these two extremes.

If the treatment is for local pain or stagnation, there will be more necessity to manipulate the needle, whereas a treatment to balance the patient's energies will require very little manipulation, as correct insertion will ensure the required effect.

Moxa and moxibustion The use of moxa is always pleasant and relaxing. It may be used in small balls placed on the
ends of the acupuncture needles, to gently heat and increase
the toning effect of the treatment, or made into small cones
and burnt directly over the skin – in which case the cone is
removed before any discomfort is felt. Larger cones may be
used indirectly, by placing a thin slice of ginger between the
moxa and the skin. This enables the cone to be burned right
down without touching the skin, and the heating qualities
of the ginger enhance the effect of the moxa.

Moxibustion may be applied to the navel (umbilicus) by
filling it with salt and placing a large cone on top of the salt.
This is often used as tonification in cases of severe depletion.

The most gentle way of using moxa is in the form of a
large cigar-shaped roll, which is lighted and moved slowly
backwards and forwards over the skin, or rotated slowly

*Moxa, the dried leaves
of the common mugwort
Artemisia vulgaris, is
used in various forms to
activate specific points
or to warm larger areas.
Here moxa sticks of
various kinds, including
a smokeless variety on
the box, are shown with
the loose herb which can
be shaped into cones and
burnt on the needle or
directly on the skin
itself.*

over an acupuncture point. This ensures gentle heating and tonification which gives a very pleasant feeling of warmth and relaxation. The moxa stick may also be used over areas of local pain, especially if the symptoms are alleviated by warmth.

The patient may be asked to use a moxa stick at home between treatments, often on the lower back or lower abdomen, to strengthen the basic energy.

The colder, damper climate of Japan has encouraged the development of moxibustion techniques. One technique frequently used in Japan is the burning of tiny 'rice grains' of moxa over specific points.

The acupuncturist moulds the moxa into small cones. These are set directly onto the skin, where they are burnt. They are taken off before they can harm the skin. Moxa burns very slowly. Used this way, the heat from the moxa can penetrate into the body. This has a very tonifying action.

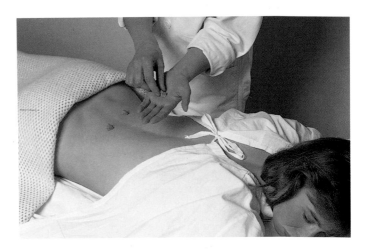

Moxa is used in several different ways, on a disc of ginger for example to increase the warming effect, or as shown here on a bed of salt in the navel, giving stimulus to the point without direct heat. This may be used in the case of severe Depletion.

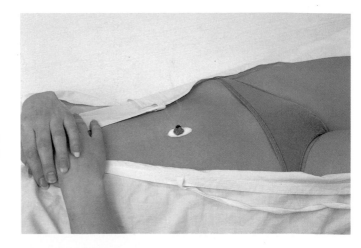

Cupping

Cupping is a traditional method of treatment used in the West as well as the East. In China, cups are usually made of glass or bamboo. A lighted taper is placed into the cup to create a vacuum: as the taper is removed the cup is quickly placed on the skin. The skin is drawn up into the cup.

Cups must be placed on an area of the body where the surface is sufficiently flat; the upper back is the most frequently chosen. The cups may also be moved up and down the back to give a more gentle stimulation to a larger area. Cupping is often used to remove Cold, and is most commonly used in cases of asthma, arthritis and the common cold.

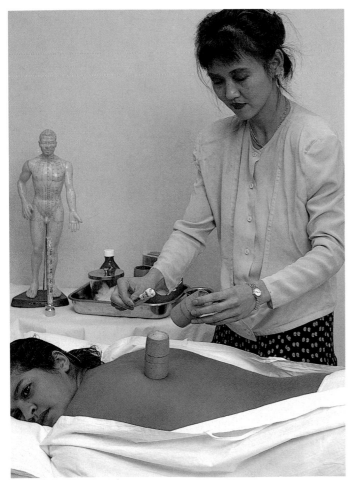

A vacuum is created in the bamboo cup by holding a flame over it to drive the oxygen out. The cup is applied to the body so creating a suction effect. Cupping is used to remove Stagnation, *in a strained or very tense muscle for example or in asthma or bronchitis from* Internal Cold. *Glass cups are also common.*

Many acupuncture points on the back are found with reference to the spinal column. Here, the practitioner feels gently between the vertebrae to check his location.

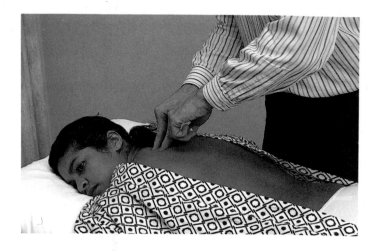

Choosing acupuncture points The choice of acupuncture points differs with each patient, and probably with each treatment, although certain points may be used repeatedly, until a particular imbalance is corrected. The points are chosen for their specific actions, and may be close to a particular area of discomfort or at some distance from it. Points on the lower leg, for example, are often chosen to treat headaches, or points on the forearm to treat problems of the chest. Sometimes, there is an obvious connection via the channels and meridians, but points may also be used for their specific action, for example, to tonify the *Blood,* to remove *Dampness,* or to strengthen digestion.

Each meridian has a series of 'command' points, which are located between the elbows and finger tips, and the

Two commonly used points: Liver 3 on the foot is used to calm the Liver Energy *and so remove* Stagnation *which produces headaches and menstrual pains; moxa on the needle at Stomach 36 restores harmony to the* Stomach *and digestion.*

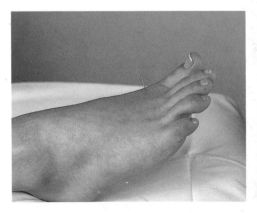

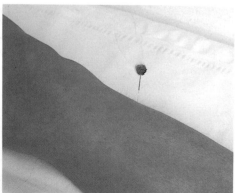

knees and toes. These points are the most frequently used in treatment as their energetic qualities are very specific and the flow of *Qi* energy in the meridians is most dynamic at the four extremities.

Five of the 'command' points on each meridian correspond to one of the five Phases: each meridian has a *Wood* point, a *Fire* point, an *Earth* point, a *Metal* point and *Water* point. These points may be chosen for their strengthening of controlling properties according to the *Sheng* and *Ke* cycles, (for example, a *Fire* point on an *Earth* meridian will be strengthening, or tonifying, as *Fire* precedes *Earth* on the *Sheng* cycle); alternatively, a *Water* point may be used to cool, an *Earth* point to ground energy.

Added to their Phase function, each of the command points is classified according to its particular energy movement: the points at the tips of the fingers and toes are called 'Well' or 'Spring' points, whereas the points located at the knees and elbows are called 'Sea' points. The flow of energy on the extremities is seen to resemble that of a river, from its springing up from the ground, to its eventual merging with the sea.

In addition to the 'command' points, specific points on the trunk relate to a particular Organ function, and also tend to be frequently used. Traditionally, there are 365 points on the body, most of which have a specific energetic function. Some are the meeting of meridian pathways, others the junction with an internal pathway of the meridian: some points tend to move energy towards the interior of the body, others bring energy to the surface. From all these diverse indications, the acupuncturist chooses a pattern of points which most suit the patient at that time, taking the pulse, the tongue and all the other methods of diagnosis into consideration.

The needles are left in place for varying lengths of time depending on the effect required, but usually the time is no more than about 15-20 minutes. Children may be treated by inserting the needle and withdrawing it almost immediately.

The pulse is taken at intervals during treatment to monitor the energy changes. There is usually an immediate change in the pulse picture as soon as the needles are inserted. If the pulse is particularly slow to respond, the practitioner may decide to use moxa to strengthen the effect of the needles.

After the needles have been removed, the pulse is taken again, to check that the balance has been restored. If the pulse responds well to the treatment, it is a good sign that the treatment will be successful.

Treatment is monitored throughout by pulse taking, to check changes in energy levels. Special attention is paid to the balance of the left and right hand pulses.

Diet and exercise When the treatment has been completed, the patient may be advised about diet or exercise, if they are relevant to the condition. Alternatively the acupuncturist may suggest certain changes in lifestyle, if it is felt that this may contribute to the cause of the imbalance.

In the West, many people suffer from stress-related prob-

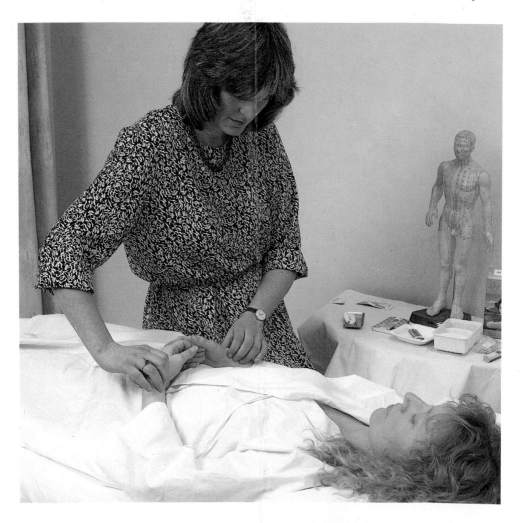

lems and, although acupuncture can help to alleviate the effects of stress on the body, the practitioner will also try to help patients to find ways of overcoming or avoiding stress in their lives. For example, simple breathing exercises practised for a short time each day can be very effective in counteracting the effects of stress. People with busy daily schedules, and especially those who are unable to bring any kind of regularity or routine to their lives, can benefit greatly from the calming effect of such breathing exercises or other relaxation techniques.

On-going treatment

After the first consultation, most patients are advised to follow a course of treatment. The duration of this always depends on the individual case, because each patient presents a different pattern. As a general rule, however, long-standing problems take longer to cure. In the East, patients with acute conditions may be seen every day, but in the West this is usually impossible. After your first visit to the acupuncturist you will usually be asked to return in a week's time, although two weeks may be more appropriate in more chronic cases.

After the complaint or illness has been improved, the patient is advised to return periodically for a check-up and to receive a treatment to prevent future imbalances. Originally, acupuncture was intended to be a preventative system of health care, and it is said that in ancient China the acupuncturist was only paid while his or her patients remained healthy! So, a visit to the acupuncturist does not have to be limited to times of illness. Traditionally, balancing treatments were given four times a year, corresponding to the change in season, in order to prepare the body for climatic changes. Because so many coughs, colds and influenza symptoms appear with the change of the weather, this kind of preventive treatment can be very beneficial.

GENERAL GUIDELINES FOR GOOD HEALTH

- Eat regularly and never hurriedly
- Live in accordance with the seasons; conserving energy in the winter months
- Express the emotions freely; do not suppress or overindulge them
- Exercise regularly, but not too strenuously

CASE HISTORIES

THE IRRITABLE CHILD

A 2-year-old girl is brought to the clinic with a tendency to skin rashes of a red, hot, itchy nature. Further investigation reveals that she has constant catarrhal problems and if ill tends to sudden high temperatures, often leading to earache. She can be a very awkward and stubborn child. Here the skin rashes are set in context of the whole case and seen as the tip of the iceberg. In Chinese terms, there is a fundamental weakness of the *Kidneys*, especially *Kidney Yin*, which allows heat to develop and take hold giving *Hot Blood*. This gives rise to the skin rashes as well as the awkward irritability of the child. The heat also injures the *Lungs* so that catarrh builds up and is not cleared. Corticosteroid skin creams for the rashes and antibiotics for the catarrh have given no longterm improvement.

The *Kidneys* are strengthened using pressure on points on the back and legs. This gives stability and calms the *Fire*, while in the acute phase points are also used to disperse the *Heat* and clear the chest. There is a dramatic period of 'clearing out' following the treatment, in which the child is sick, throws up catarrh, has smelly diarrhoea and yellow discharges from the eyes and ears. This temporary phase is followed by a restoration of vitality and a marked improvement in health and temperament generally. Both skin and chest become clear.

THE ECZEMA BABY

A child of 16 months is brought to the clinic by his parents. He is alert and lively, but his face is pale, with bright red cheeks which look sore and chapped. There is yellow mucus at the nostrils. Further examination shows that the skin on his arms and back is also very dry and irritated. The glands in his neck are swollen and his breath does not smell fresh.

Questioning the parents reveals that from the age of eight months, the child's bowels have been very loose, and he has had a constantly runny nose. He had been breastfed up to seven months, and until that time he had no illness. Though the parents are healthy, there is some asthma in the father's family.

It is difficult to take the pulse of children under three years of age, though the acupuncturist detects a 'wiry' quality in both middle positions, relating to digestive function.

From the presenting symptoms, the practitioner guesses correctly that very soon after the breastfeeding was stopped the child had a sudden growth spurt and also had a series of immunizations. The combination of these three factors proved too much for the child's digestive function. A condition of internal *Heat* was created, which showed itself as an eczema-type skin condition.

Special points on the fingers – used particularly to strengthen childrens' digestion – are chosen for the first treatment. The needles are inserted and almost immediately withdrawn. A herbal medicine is also prescribed.

The child responds quickly to the treatment and from the first visit the runny nose improves. After one month the skin is noticably better and continues to improve.

This case is very typical of many young children, and if treated at the time of onset can prevent the occurrence of asthma/eczema conditions in later life.

THE HAY FEVER VICTIM

A businessman in his 20s comes with 'hay-fever'. He is affected as the weather gets hotter in the summer, gets a very blocked nose to the point where it is difficult for him to talk and has red itchy eyes which can be crusted over and stuck together after sleeping. He has tried all medication without success.

Chinese diagnosis reveals a weakness of the *Lungs* and *Kidneys* with a tendency for the *Liver Fire* to rise with business stress or heat, so raising the mucus to the head. Treatment is given to points locally around the nose, and elsewhere to strengthen the *Lungs* and *Kidneys*, while calming the *Liver* energy.

The nose clears in treatment and with further sessions is much improved during the summer. He returns in winter for preventive treatment and improves further each year.

CASE HISTORIES

THE COMPULSIVE EATER

A.young woman of 19 comes to the clinic. She says she is obsessed about her weight and with eating. There are times when she cannot stop eating, then she makes herself vomit. She is also worried about her periods which started at the age of 14 but only comes every 6 months. She is lonely and depressed but feels much better in and after her period. In Chinese terms, there is a fundamental imbalance in the *Earth* element – an unwillingness to accept nourishment – and in the *Chong Mai*, an extraordinary meridian concerned with the nourishment of the womb and the onset of periods. The lack of nourishment from food contributes to the menstruation being very infrequent.

Treatment is given to stabilize the *Earth* and regulate *Chong Mai* using especially points on the legs on the *Spleen* meridian and points on the lower abdomen. The next period comes after 6 weeks and the desire to overeat and make herself vomit is lessening. The following period comes in 4 weeks and from then on the cycle is regulated.

In this case normalizing the periods re-establishes normal eating habits. In Chinese terms, the two are often interrelated.

THE HIGH FLYER

The patient enters the room with quick movements: he is assertive and friendly. His complexion is slightly flushed. He complains of stomach pains, which he feels are stress-related. He has a very demanding job, involving many late night meetings and business lunches. Recently his sleep has been affected and he has headaches, usually at the sides of the head.

The pulse is fast and wiry especially in the *Wood* position. The tongue is slightly red at the sides. *Wood* energy tends to ascend, causing both the headaches and the inability to 'wind down' in order to sleep. Points are chosen on the *Liver* and *Gallbladder* meridians to cool the *Liver Fire* and pull the energy down from the head and to strengthen the *Yin* of the *Liver*. Other points are chosen for their calming effect, particularly on the digestive system.

The patient is advised to avoid alcohol and fried foods, which create *Heat* in the *Liver* and *Gallbladder*. As it is not possible for the patient to change his lifestyle at the present time, he is advised to devote a short time each day to meditation or deep breathing exercises to relieve stress. Within a few weeks his stomach pains have disappeared, his headaches occur only occasionally, and his sleep has improved.

THE ASTHMATIC ATHLETE

A middle-aged man, athletic in appearance, comes to the clinic with asthma, which he has had for three years. He is good natured with a fine sense of humour. He is still an active sportsman, but relies more and more on medication to control his breathing. He has a cough, which is worse at night.

Asked about the onset of his problem, he remembers that nine months before the first attack he was hospitalized for a low back injury which slightly damaged his right kidney. Soon after he was released from hospital, he caught a very severe chill, and had to stay in bed for a few days.

The pulse was very tight and deep, and in the third position on the left side, weak. The tongue slightly pale, with white fur. This indicates a pattern of *Cold*, and a weak *Kidney* function.

In Chinese Medicine, the *Lung* and the *Kidneys* have a special relationship and damage to one will always affect the other. If the *Kidney* energy is impaired, the *Lung* energy can stagnate laying the *Lungs* open to attack from *External Cold*.

The practitioner decides to use cupping on the points relating to the *Lungs* on the upper back. This will remove the *Cold* and stagnation. He also uses acupuncture on points to strengthen the *Lung* and *Kidney* function. Moxa cones are burnt on the lower back.

The acupuncturist advises the patient to rest: he has a demanding job, and spends much of his leisure time pursuing active sports. He is also advised to restrict his sexual activity until his *Kidney* function is sufficiently strengthened. With treatment there is steady improvement in the asthma. After a few months the patient can leave off all medication.

CASE HISTORIES

THE ARTHRITIC

A woman of 45 comes diagnosed as having rheumatoic arthritis. Her joints – especially the wrist and fingers – puff up and get hot and red. They are painful and very weak so that she often drops things. She has had two major operations – a thyroidectomy 20 years ago and a hysterectomy 9 years ago. The hospital put her on an extensive course of anti-inflammatory tablets which upset her stomach. She is overweight, tired and depressed, loves rich foods, sauces and wine.

Her tongue has a thick yellow coating and the pulse is deep and slippery. This is a complex case but one of the central factors is a weakening of the *Spleen*, leading to a tendency to accumulate *Damp* which turns to *Heat* through stagnation. This has blocked the movement of the joints.

Dietary advice to cut down on cream, cheese, red meat, rich spicy foods and alcohol was given and points used to re-establish the flow of *Qi* both locally and generally as well as clearing the *Damp* and *Heat*.

As treatment progressed the joints improved steadily, the patient substantially helping herself with the improved diet. Even when the hands were quite free of pain and stiffness the patient returned for three-monthly checkups to prevent recurrence.

THE MOTHER

The patient arrives at the clinic wearing lots of clothes, has a pale complexion and a quiet voice. She complains of low back ache which has bothered her since the birth of her last child. She also has little control of her bladder, waking up at least twice in the night to pass water. Recently she has felt no interest in sex and has frequent diarrhoea with no pain but containing undigested food.

The pulse is deep and weak especially in the third position on the right wrist, relating to *Kidney Yang*. The tongue is pale and moist and slightly swollen. She dislikes cold, and finds that a hot water bottle on her lower back or lower abdomen makes her feel better.

The acupuncturist diagnoses *Kidney Yang Deficiency* leading to *Spleen Yang Deficiency* and *Internal Cold*. The patient has had three children at very close intervals, which has not given her body enough time to recover sufficient energy in between pregnancies. This has caused a depletion of *Kidney Yang*, the generative force, which together with a diet of almost completely raw foods, has led to a *Spleen Yang Deficiency* and *Internal Cold*.

Treatment aims to warm and tonify, using needles and moxa. Points relating to the *Kidneys* on the lower back are tonified by burning moxa cones, as are points on the lower abdomen (Conception Vessel 3 and 4) to strengthen the *Bladder* and to tonify the *Lower Heater* and the uterus.

The patient is advised against a raw food diet: the diarrhoea with undigested food suggesting a *Spleen Yang Deficiency* with the inability to absorb food. Slightly cooked or steamed vegetables are more easily digested and give the necessary warmth to the body.

Treatment once a week for six weeks shows a marked improvement. The patient feels much happier, and more able to cope with her young family.

THE EPILEPTIC

A man in his 40s comes to the clinic with constant congestion in the sinuses. During case taking the acupuncturist discovers that he has had regular epileptic attacks from an early age which come on especially after stimulation or excitement. He has taken medication for this for years.

The acupuncturist assesses that *Kidney* and *Liver Yin* are weak. This allows *Liver Wind* to develop inside when the *Liver* energy is stimulated too strongly. In Chinese terms the *Liver Wind* stirs up excess *Phlegm* which moves upwards, clouding the mind and confusing the senses. This leads to an epileptic attack. Treatment is given to clear the *Phlegm* and calm the *Liver* by strengthening the *Kidneys* and drawing excess *Qi* down from the head. The sinus problem clears quite quickly. Over a period of many months the medication for epilepsy is reduced and the fits become less frequent and less severe.

6

RELATED
THERAPIES

Many of the so-called 'alternative' therapies may be seen to be related to acupuncture because they recognize and use the body's more subtle energies. Those specifically described in this chapter have a particular relationship, in that they use the principles of oriental diagnosis, and recognize the flow of energy through the meridians.

Nevertheless, it is possible that some therapies which do not formally acknowledge the existence of the meridians may nevertheless be using them unconsciously. This idea was borne out when acupuncturists from Japan visited the faith healers of the Philippines and noted that they were often using particular acupuncture points as the site for their 'psychic surgery'. In the West, the many 'hand healers' may also be affecting the flow of energy in the meridians.

Herbalism

In China, acupuncture and herbalism go hand in hand. Hospitals of traditional Chinese medicine provide not only acupuncture and moxibustion, but also the prescription of Chinese herbs, general and specific dietary advice, and massage. In the West, however, Chinese herbalism is practised mostly within local Chinese communities, although there are definite signs that this is changing. In parts of USA herbalism is now a required part of training.

In the past, the practice of Chinese herbalism outside China has been inhibited by the difficulty of finding specific herbs. A further deterrent to Westerners is that, even if a Chinese herbal dispensary can be located, prescriptions can only be fulfilled if they are written in Chinese. Nowadays, however, a growing awareness of the importance placed on herbs in traditional oriental medicine is encouraging acupuncturists to study Chinese herbalism and post-graduate study courses on the prescription of herbs have recently become available. This will provide a new generation of practitioners who are equipped with the skills of both acupuncture and herbalism; in the meantime, Chinese herbal dispensaries are getting used to being visited by an increasing number of Westerners.

A visit to a herbalist

A typical herbal dispensary is stocked from floor to ceiling with an enormous variety of herbal medicines. These include not only an extraordinary variety of plants, but also such oddities as deer antler or cow's gallstones, all of which are displayed in large glass bottles or in row after row of glass-fronted drawers. Some dispensaries do no more than fulfil prescriptions, while others have a resident Chinese doctor who is available for consultation.

Visiting a herbalist is similar in many ways to visiting an acupuncturist. All Chinese herbalists have a thorough knowledge of acupuncture, and the basis of diagnosis is exactly the same. The pulse is taken. The tongue is observed. Questions are asked about the history of the complaint, the patient's likes and dislikes, and so on. The practitioner will observe the patient carefully in exactly the same way as an acupuncturist would do prior to treatment. Indeed, it is probable that the doctor will not have decided at this stage whether herbalism or acupuncture or treatment with both is required.

A miniaturized version of a traditional Chinese herbalist's shop, dispensing herbal medicines and potions. In traditional Chinese medicine, herbalism and acupuncture go hand in hand, and Chinese-trained acupuncturists spend at least two years of their course making a thorough study of herbalism.

If herbal treatment is decided upon, the practitioner carefully makes out a prescription. This is a meticulous procedure, because at least five and sometimes as many as twenty different herbs may be chosen for their individual and combined effects. The prescription is then taken to the dispensary for the most fascinating part of the visit – weighing and dividing the herbs.

Each herb in the prescription is taken from its drawer, weighed carefully, and divided into equal portions for each daily dose. Sliced stems, slivers of bark, twigs, leaves, dried flowers, and powdered roots are all piled together or tied up in separate bundles. When the herbs for the prescription have been sorted in this way, the herbalist writes down precise instructions for making infusions of the herbs. These must be followed carefully, because the infusion process can be complicated, often requiring prolonged boiling until only a precise amount of liquid remains.

Drinking the prepared liquid is likely to be the most unpleasant part of the process. Chinese medicinal herbs tend to have strong, bitter tastes. However, the taste seems to improve the more a preparation is drunk – there often seems to be a perceptible sense of vitality and healthiness in the flavour, more than the feeling that anything tasting so bad must be doing some good.

How herbs work

While acupuncture works by affecting and moving the body's energy, herbs work more materially. In cases of severe constitutional depletion, for example, a practitioner would tend to use herbs to build up the patient's constitution before using acupuncture.

Although the prescription of herbs is based on exactly the same methods of diagnosis as acupuncture, the herbalist places even more emphasis on the Eight Principle Patterns of *Yin* and *Yang*. The action of herbs is often described in active terms – for example, 'warming and invigorating', 'cooling and calming', or more specifically, 'removing *Damp* from the *Spleen*', or 'cooling *Heat* in the *Stomach*'.

The action of herbs in Western terms

Like other aspects of Chinese medicine, herbalism has been exposed in recent years to the scrutiny of Western medical research. As might be expected, many of the plants used in herbal prescriptions have been found to contain similar chemicals to those that are used to treat the same conditions in orthodox medicine. This is not particularly surprising, because many Western pharmaceuticals have herbal origins. More interesting is the fact that analysis of certain plants used in herbal remedies has found that they contain several active ingredients which actually complement each other to make their combined effect either safer or more potent (or possibly both) than would be the effect of single active ingredients used alone.

The common foxglove (*Digitalis purpurea*), a natural source from which pharmacologists isolate the drug called digitalis, is commonly used in the treatment of heart conditions. Interestingly, foxglove has also been found to contain a chemical called verodoxin, which reinforces the effect of digitalis and therefore allows smaller doses to be used when the two are combined than are required if digitalis is used alone.

Similarly, dandelion (*Taraxacum officinale*) has diuretic properties, but also contains large amounts of potassium, which is lost by anyone taking diuretics – and so is naturally replaced if the diuretic used is natural dandelion rather than a chemical isolated from it.

Dandelion
*(*Taraxacum officinale*)*

In general, herbs tend to have a slower and more gentle effect than refined chemicals used as drugs. Although sometimes the precision and rapid action of a refined drug is necessary to treat specific conditions, the more gradual action of herbs seems to be preferable for long-term treatment of chronic conditions.

Another curious property of some herbal treatments is that their action seems to redress an imbalance, or regulate the organism, rather than to have a specific, 'stimulus-response' type of effect. In this they seem to act in a similar way to acupuncture points. In Western terms, we think of a drug being prescribed in order to produce a single specific reaction. If the opposite reaction is required, a different drug is needed. This does not necessarily seem to be the case with herbal remedies, however. For example, the root of angelica (*Angelica archangelica*) can have a dual action on the womb (uterus), relaxing it when it is tight and contracting it when it is slack.

Two-way actions of this kind are quite common among herbal remedies, and such regulatory effects are central to the concepts of balance and harmony that lie at the heart of Chinese medical theory.

Angelica
*(*Angelica archangelica*)*

Diet

Any person's state of health depends on how they live and also on what they eat. Acupuncturists in China place considerable emphasis on diet, therefore, and advise their patients accordingly. This advice does not focus on calorie counts or vitamin contents of food, however, but rather on the food's balancing and energizing qualities. Some hospitals in China even have a special restaurant attached to them, where patients can have their food prescriptions made up to suit their individual requirements.

Some foods are considered to be 'warming'; others to be 'cooling', and a patient will be advised to eat certain foods and avoid others, depending on the diagnosis. Each food is also considered to have a specific 'taste', described in similar terms to our Western understanding of the word, but with a special significance from a Chinese medical point of view.

These 'tastes' are divided according to the Five Phases into *Sour, Bitter, Sweet, Pungent* and *Salty*, and are classified in this way in the Table of Correspondences (p.62-3). It is considered to be important to include all the 'tastes' within each meal, because each 'taste' nourishes a particular organic system. Taken in excess, however, a 'taste' can damage the same organ it would normally nourish. As with all aspects of Chinese medicine, diet is a matter of balance.

Macrobiotics

Although the macrobiotic dietary system originated in Japan, it is based on exactly the same principles as those applied to diet in China. In the West it has tended to be misunderstood and consequently distorted by being taken to unhealthy extremes. Practised by an experienced therapist, however, macrobiotics can be used effectively both to increase health and to treat disease.

In treating a disease, an extreme form of diet may be required temporarily in order to cleanse and purify the system. Even in relative health, the occasional cleansing regime – for example, a diet consisting only of unrefined rice – may also be beneficial. On the other hand, it is totally against the principles of oriental medicine to maintain this kind of diet for long periods of time. As with every other form of Oriental therapy, the rules of balance and living in harmony with nature apply.

Macrobiotics shares the same concern for balancing the five 'tastes', and for balancing different kinds of foods:

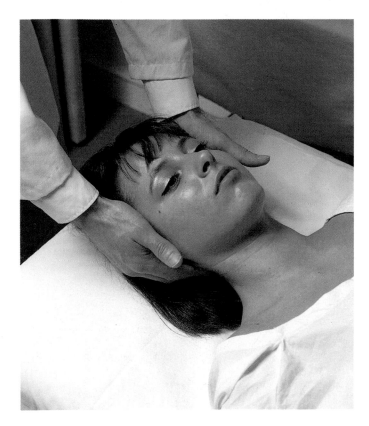

Massage has long been a soothing and effective therapy in both West and East. Traditionally, acupuncturists are also trained in massage which they sometimes use in conjunction with needling.

grains, vegetables, fruits and nuts. Dairy produce and meats are kept to a minimum, and meat when eaten is always combined with vegetables and grains. In order to keep in harmony with nature, foods are ideally eaten only in their season. Where possible locally produced foods are preferred, because food that grows in the same environment as the one in which we live is considered to provide the nutrients that we need most.

Massage

Many kinds of massage are used in conjunction with traditional treatments in the East. Some work on muscles and other tissues; some concentrate on the meridians, to help the body's energy flow; and some focus on the acupuncture points. In the West the most frequently encountered massage therapy is Shiatsu, a variant of which is also called acupressure.

Shiatsu

Developed in Japan at the beginning of the twentieth century, Shiatsu unites ancient forms of oriental massage with modern Western techniques of both Swedish massage and manipulation.

Chinese medicine was introduced into Japan more than 1,000 years ago. At that time massage was an integral part of the healing system, and was used for many years as a therapy alongside other forms of Chinese medicine. Over the last two centuries massage as a therapy went into decline and was used only 'for pleasure and comfort' rather than as a therapeutic technique.

The development of Shiatsu was partly a revitalization of these ancient techniques, although it also included the use of very sophisticated diagnostic methods. Nowadays in Japan, Shiatsu (as practised by an experienced practitioner, with a full knowledge of oriental medical theory and diagnosis)

Although a youthful therapy compared to the ancient art of acupuncture, Shiatsu (developed in Japan at the beginning of the 20th century) has become firmly established as an effective means of treatment. Shiatsu works by exerting pressure on the acunpuncture points and along the merdians to stimulate the flow of Qi or energy.

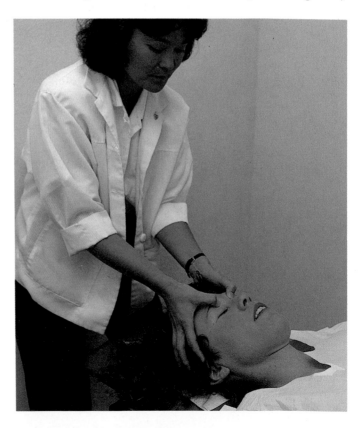

ranks alongside acupuncture and medical herbalism as an effective form of treatment.

The professional Shiatsu practitioner is expected to have a thorough knowledge of the points and meridians of acupuncture (in Shiatsu, the acupuncture points are known as *Tsubo*) and the subtleties of pulse and tongue diagnosis. In Shiatsu, however, abdominal or *Hara* diagnosis is particularly developed, and some schools concentrate almost exclusively on this form of diagnosis. Shizuto Masunaga, the founder of the school of Zen Shiatsu says:

> 'The Hara *is the source of* Ki *energy. All diseases stem from this area. Therefore you can feel everything by diagnosing the* Hara'.

This emphasis on the *Hara* and the *Ki* (Japanese for *Qi*) is common to most Japanese therapies, and is also important in the practice of all kinds of martial arts. In Shiatsu, as with many martial arts, energy is directed from the *Hara* into the hands by concentration and regulation of the breath. It is this concentration on breathing – and even more on the direction of energy by means of breathing – that sets Shiatsu apart from other forms of massage. The breath is also used to establish a flow of energy between the patient and the practitioner.

There are many levels of Shiatsu practice, and in Japan nearly everyone practises some form of Shiatsu or massage, from the level of 'home remedy' massage of the shoulders and neck to relieve tension and fatigue, to the fully-trained professional therapist.

Unlike acupuncture, which requires a full training in oriental medicine before a person is allowed to practise, Shiatsu may be practised at any level with good effect, if the student learns the fundamental skills of breath control. Simple meridian stretches and massage along the course of the meridians can be a highly effective, all-over treatment, although more specific problems need the skills of a qualified practitioner. In the West there are now a number of schools that offer three-year, part-time courses leading to a professional certificate, as well as several classes for laymen.

Attending a good course in Shiatsu is probably the best introduction to oriental medicine, because it teaches the student the fundamental skills required to strengthen and balance his or her *Qi* and to develop concentration.

Exercise

In China and Japan, exercise is taken very seriously. Early in the morning Chinese parks are crowded with people of all ages practising Tai Ji Juan (often written Tai Chi Chuan, and referred to simply as Tai Ji or Tai Chi), or one of the many other related forms of exercise. In Japan, office workers start each day's work by lining up beside their desks to perform simple sets of exercises that improve their energy flow and regulate the functioning of their internal organs. The companies that encourage this evidently believe that the advantage they derive from the improved health of their employees makes the time spent doing these exercises a worthwhile investment.

Tai Ji Juan and Qi Gong

When practised in their purest form, many martial arts are closely related to oriental medicine in their understanding of energy flow and the balance of *Yin* and *Yang*. In fact, in many parts of the East it was masters of the various martial arts who kept oriental medicine alive during times of decline and persecution. Furthermore, several Japanese martial arts actually include a knowledge of acupuncture points as part of training.

But it is the Chinese forms of Tai Ji and Qi Gong that are particularly relevant to medicine. This is because they are both widely used specifically for their therapeutic effects and are often prescribed in China as part of a patient's treatment.

Qi Gong, in particular, was developed for its benefits to health and has been part of Chinese medicine for more than 3,000 years. It is considered to be an effective means of medical treatment in itself, and exercises have been developed to treat specific conditions. In classic texts, Qi Gong is called, 'the method to eliminate disease and to prolong life'.

Qi Gong consists of repeating quite simple exercises and success depends on mental attitude, correct posture, correct breathing and perseverance. The same exercises have to be done again and again in order to have the required effect, and in some hospitals in China, where Qi Gong has been successfully used in the treatment of cancer, patients may practise for at least four hours each morning.

In order to understand the effectiveness of Qi Gong, it is important to accept the idea that matter is not static, but is always in a state of change; that matter is in fact a condensa-

Now becoming known in the West, Qi Gong *has long been established in China as an effective medical therapy, which actively eliminates the disease and promotes long life. It is based on a series of simple movements which must be practised regularly with correct breath control and mental concentration.*

Tai Ji Juan, or Tai Chi as it is usually known, is a martial art, but one based on the development of inner strength as a means of self-defence. Tai Ji Juan exercises have a distinctive flowing pattern based on the perfect strength and harmony of a circle.

tion of energy. It is not inert and it can be altered. Chinese medicine assumes that there is energetic interchange between matter and energy. In the same way, the breath may be used and directed to affect the material structures of the body. Nevertheless, deriving benefit is a slow process, which requires a great deal of perseverance!

Tai Ji Juan may be seen as a more gentle and preventive therapy, although it is no less effective if practised diligently. It is particularly valuable in maintaining balance and a good flow of energy through the meridians and organs. It calms the mind by regulation of the breathing and helps to unify mind and body by concentration on the movements of the exercises.

Through a series of flowing exercises, originating in the fighting forms of the martial arts, Tai Ji attempts to harmonize *Yin* and *Yang*, fullness and emptiness, hardness and softness, within the body. Its forms are based on the circle, to give maximum strength and stability with the minimum of strain. The circle symbolizes harmony, and Tai Ji encourages smoothness and pliability. A Chinese proverb observes that 'the willow does not break under the snow', implying that strength can be found in flexibility.

Tai Ji Juan is now becoming more accessible in the West, and interest in Qi Gong is rapidly increasing. A patient receiving acupuncture treatment may be advised to practise Tai Ji as a method of maintaining the balance brought about by the acupuncture. Its calming and regulatory effects are particularly beneficial to those who suffer from stress and tension.

Meditation

In the East, meditation is not seen primarily as something mystical. It is valued as a proven and practical aid to calming the mind and the body, in order to improve the functions of both.

Aids to meditation include breathing exercises, focusing the attention on particular areas of the body, or simply calming the mind. All of these are commonly used as a part of daily life by many people in both China and Japan and as part of normal health maintenance. In this way – as another aspect of the general system of oriental medicine and health care – meditation complements acupuncture in a direct and practical way.

The calm faces of these young Buddhist monks demonstrate the effectiveness of meditation. Meditation in its many forms has been used for thousands of years by spiritual communities all over the world to clear the mind and aid concentration. Properly practised, it focuses the mind and regulates the body, increasing purposeful and effective participation in life.

7

FOUNDATIONS OF ACUPUNCTURE

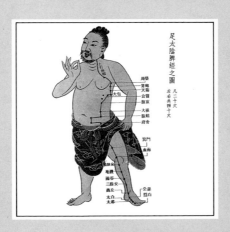

The origins of acupuncture are impossible to define because they lie in periods before recorded history. Stone needles have been found in ancient tombs in Inner Mongolia, dating from the Neolithic Era (*c.* 2,500 BC). Bronze, gold and silver needles have been recovered from later tombs. Writings on silk scrolls describing 11 channels and their treatment with moxibustion have been found in tombs dating from the Han dynasty (*c.* 200 BC).

The first written account of acupuncture treatment occurs in the *Shi Ji* –'Historical records' – (*c.* 200 BC) which tells of Bia Que, a doctor in the fourth century BC, who was famous for bringing a prince out of a coma by means of acupuncture. Bia Que also systematized the Four Methods of Diagnosis: Observing; Listening and Smelling; Asking; and Touching.

Confucius (Kong Fu Zi) (551-479 BC).

Chinese medicine: a brief history

The whole theory of Chinese medicine, with its emphasis on *Qi*, evolved out of an era of philosophical speculation and intense consideration of the nature of life. It is no coincidence that great thinkers such as Kong Fu Zi (Confucius), Lao Zi, Meng Zi, and Zhuang Zi preceded the great classic of Chinese medicine, the *Huang Di Nei Jing* – 'The Yellow Emperor's Classic of Internal Medicine' – which was compiled between 300 and 100 BC. While neither a Daoist nor a Confucian text, it draws on both their traditions and perspectives. The Daoist philosophers in particular, who were masters of the simple and essential, have always been known for their interest, not only in the nature of reality, but also the maintenance and improvement of vitality through specific exercises and techniques such as meditation, breathing, and massage. The *Nei Jing*, as it is more usually known, is divided into two parts: the first part, *Su Wen* – 'Essential Questions' – is more theoretical; the second part, *Ling Shu* – 'Spiritual Pivot' – is more practical. It remains even today the foundation work for the theory and philosophy behind Chinese medicine.

Ivory figures of two of the mythical founders of Chinese medicine: Huang Di, the Yellow Emperor, with Shen Nong.

Set in a conversation form between Huang Di, the Yellow Emperor, and his minister Qi Bo and others, the *Nei Jing* outlines the principles of natural law and the movements of life – *Yin/Yang; Wu Xing* (the Five Phases); the interrelationship between Heaven, Earth and Man; *Zang-Fu* (the Organ system); *Jing-Luo* (the meridian network); *Qi* and *Blood*; and the causes of disease, their effects, diagnosis

A Song dynasty painting showing a country doctor applying moxibustion to the back. Even today in China and Japan moxa scars can sometimes be seen on older patients. This is not common in the West where moxibustion is used gently and painlessly.

and treatment. It gives the basis of the Eight Principles and the later differentiation of syndromes, describes the nine kinds of needle and their use, and emphasizes preventive treatment. It is a rich source book that is still used by acupuncturists today, 2000 years after it was written, in combination with the many later texts that exist as commentaries and amplifications of it.

The first real clinical text on traditional Chinese medicine – the *Shang Han Lun*, or 'Treatise on Febrile Diseases', was written by Zhang Zhong Jing in about AD 210. It provides a systematic presentation, diagnosis and treatment of various acute fevers, including typhoid, cholera and dysentery, and discusses a theory about the progression of fevers that is still used today.

Huang Fu Mi's classic of acupuncture and moxibustion, which includes the accurate location of 349 points, appeared around the same time. This was used in 1979 (1,700 years later) in the preparation of the important modern work *Essentials of Acupuncture,* compiled by the major acupuncture colleges of China. This kind of use of previous material is typical in acupuncture – the emphasis is always on building upon the firm foundations of the past. The *Mai Jing* 'Pulse Classic', giving a systematic and detailed description of diagnosis by the pulse – another of the keystones of Chinese medicine – was also written in the third century AD.

Through the centuries following the publication of these seminal works, acupuncture developed, often within a family, with sons serving as apprentices to their fathers. In the Tang Dynasty (618-907 AD) medical academies were established and in about 1026 the *Classic of the Bronze Man* was written, an illustrated guide to points as shown on two life-size bronze acupuncture figures. This became a standard work and was engraved on two stone tablets more than two metres high and seven metres wide that were kept in the capital.

As dynasty succeeded dynasty, many more important works were published. In the Ming Dynasty (1368-1644), the famous Chinese herbalist Li Shi Zhen published his 50-volume *Compendium of Materia Medica* as well as a study of the Pulse and the Extraordinary Meridians.

Acupuncture and Western medicine in China

The Qing Dynasty (1644-1911) saw a decline in acupuncture and herbalism, however. This coincided with the increasing influence of Western ideas in China, and in 1822 a government decree actually banned the practice of acupuncture from the Imperial Medical College, because undressing (even for medical examination) was considered improper. In Republican China (1911-1949) the Kuomintang government tried to ban traditional medicine in 1929, but there were so many protests from traditional doctors that the attempt failed. However, acupuncture seems to have survived less well in the cities than in the country at this time.

After Liberation and the establishment of the People's Republic in 1949, there was a great resurgence of interest in acupuncture at a national level, especially in combining its use with Western medicine. Books and papers were

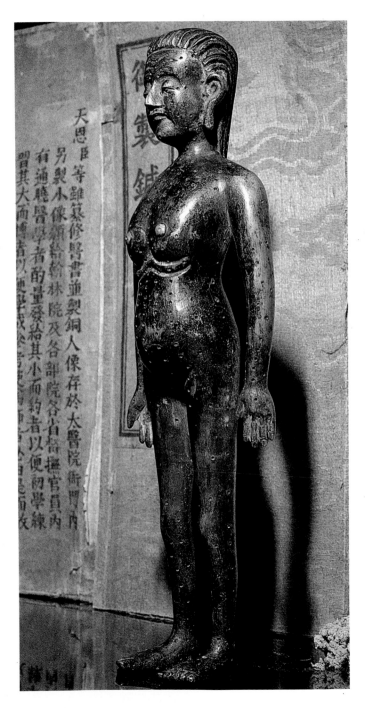

A bronze teaching figure used to familiarize acupuncture students with the positions of the acupuncture points along the meridians. Each point is indicated by a tiny needle-sized hole. When working on a flesh-and-blood patient, however, acupuncturists always feel for the points. They are never in precisely the same place, because we are not all exactly the same size, shape and proportion.

published, acupuncture departments were established in hospitals, and a thorough modernization and systematization of old methods was carried out. Investigations were also made into ear, finger, nose, face and scalp needling.

Around 1958, acupuncture began to become renowned for its effectiveness in pain control. At first it was primarily used in this way for post-operative care, but later it was introduced for anaesthesia during operations. Experimentation started with minor operations such as tooth extraction, then was extended to tonsillectomy, thyroidectomy, repair of hernias and finally to major operations on the limbs, thorax and abdomen.

This dramatic use of acupuncture caught the Western imagination, but unfortunately also led to the widespread misconception that acupuncture's effectiveness was limited only to pain control and anaesthesia.

During the Cultural Revolution (1966-1976), following the persecution of surgeons and doctors practising Western medicine, traditional Chinese medicine – being the original national medicine – was given new opportunities to develop. Hospitals and training centres for traditional Chinese medicine were established throughout the country. At the same time, however, because of the extraordinary social upheaval of this period, when religions were banned, temples smashed and traditions overturned, traditional theories were often rejected and many new methods tried. These included needle-embedding, point-injection, electrical acupuncture and analgesia. Exaggerated claims were common and abuses of the usual guidelines – such as very deep needling used at traditionally forbidden points – were also practised.

Since 1975, China has opened its doors once more to the world. Three-month advanced courses on acupuncture, supported by the World Health Organization, are now offered to foreigners in major cities such as Beijing, Guangzhou, Nanjing, and Shanghai. The emphasis is on clinical practice because previous training is assumed.

In China a full training in traditional Chinese medicine entails five years of study. This includes Chinese herbalism, a major topic with exactly the same theoretical base as acupuncture. On such a course, approximately 30 per cent of the teaching concerns orthodox clinical sciences (such as anatomy, physiology and pathology). The seriousness with which acupuncture is now regarded is indicated in this

In China today patients have a choice of Western or traditional Chinese medicine. Here a Chinese worker is treated with traditional means – acupuncture and moxibustion.

lengthy training, and the status of an acupuncturist is the same as that of a doctor trained in Western medicine.

Today acupuncture is used far more extensively in China than in the West, in a hospital-based system with facilities for in- as well as out-patients, and for treating acute as well as chronic cases. The national policy is to pursue both systems side by side with extensive clinical research. Patients have the choice of both Western or traditional Chinese medicine and evidently seem to benefit from both. This idea of extending choice to the patient may well spread to other countries in the future.

Acupuncture in other countries

The place of acupuncture in many Far Eastern countries – such as Japan, Korea, and Malaysia – is similar to that in China itself. The Soviet Union has also been using and researching acupuncture since its renewed contact with the Chinese in the 1950s. Since this time its use has increased steadily and, in 1972, acupuncture clinics were planned for all the major medical centres in the Soviet Union. It is used not only for pain control but also for treating a wide variety of conditions including asthma, stomach ulcers, raised blood pressure and angina.

The practice of acupuncture has, of course, continued throughout the world in the many thriving expatriate Chinese communities.

Acupuncture is also becoming more firmly established in Australia with government recognition of training courses, and acceptance of registered practitioners by health insurance companies.

Acupuncture in the USA

Until the 1970s, acupuncture in the USA was largely confined to the oriental quarters of major American cities. However, since 1971, development has been substantial. Books and articles have appeared by the dozen, practitioners have come from China, Japan and Korea and theorists and teachers have also visited from Europe. Americans in greater numbers have began to study acupuncture and schools of acupuncture have been established in various parts of the country. Many states now recognize the medical and therapeutic value of acupuncture. Acupuncturists are licensed for independent practice in fifteen states – California, Florida, Hawaii, Montana, Nevada, New Mexico, New York, New Jersey, Oregon, Rhode Island and Washington; four other states (Maryland, Massachusetts, Pennsylvania and Utah) as well as the District of Columbia license acupuncturists to work in collaboration with other physicians.

State recognition reflects the amount of research being carried out at centres such as the University of California, Downstate Medical Center New York, Upstate Medical Center in Rochester NJ, the Lemuel Shattuck Teaching Hospital in Boston and the University of Virginia.

Since 1981, the unifying force in American acupuncture has been the American Association for Acupuncture and Oriental Medicine (AAAOM) which serves both as a forum for the profession and an advocate for new thought and directions. In 1982, the National Accreditation Commission for Schools and Colleges of Acupuncture and Oriental Medicine was set up as an independent body to monitor the performance, integrity and quality of the acupuncture teaching establishments in the USA.

Acupuncture is steadily growing in the USA; there are some 4,000 practitioners currently at work and at least 300 new ones are accredited each year.

Acupuncture in Europe

The earliest references to acupuncture in Europe are found in the seventeenth century. At this time it was viewed more as a curiosity than a system of medicine, however. Its use is recorded at the Paris medical school in 1810, where a Dr Berlioz used it to treat a young woman suffering with abdominal pain. He claimed to have had great success with acupuncture, especially in treating neurogenic diseases. Nevertheless, it was not widely adopted by his colleagues.

In Britain there have been similar occasional uses of acupuncture recorded from the early nineteenth century, but these did not lead to any significantly sustained interest.

The development of acupuncture in Europe this century was given its initial impetus largely by Dr Soulie de Morant's *L'Acupuncture Chinoise*, published in 1929, which he used as a text to teach traditional acupuncture to French medical practitioners. Much of his teaching came directly from the *Zhen Jiu Da Cheng*, the seventeenth-century Chinese *Compendium of Acupuncture*. He contributed greatly to the recognition of acupuncture in France as an important part of the art and science of medicine.

In Britain serious study of traditional acupuncture did not develop until the 1950s and early 1960s. The links were either through France of from direct contact with teachers and schools in Taiwan, Korea or elsewhere in the Far East. Translations from the Chinese medical classics also became more easily available. Although a Medical Acupuncture Society was set up, its members generally ignored traditional theory as being outdated and incomprehensible.

The serious students of acupuncture came from the ranks of those who were already interested in or actually practising natural medicine – osteopaths, homeopaths and naturopaths. For them, the Chinese ideas about medicine – although of course expressed in different terms – were similar to much of what they had already been practising. Ideas such as the treatment of individuals rather than of a separately identified disease; treatment of the whole rather than the part; and a belief in the value of the body's own restorative powers as the key to curing disease, rather than in the suppression of symptoms. To many it seemed that traditional Chinese medicine had formalized and set down in terms of *Yin/Yang*, the Five Phases, the Eight Principles, and so on, many of the concepts they had found from their own experience, or knew instinctively.

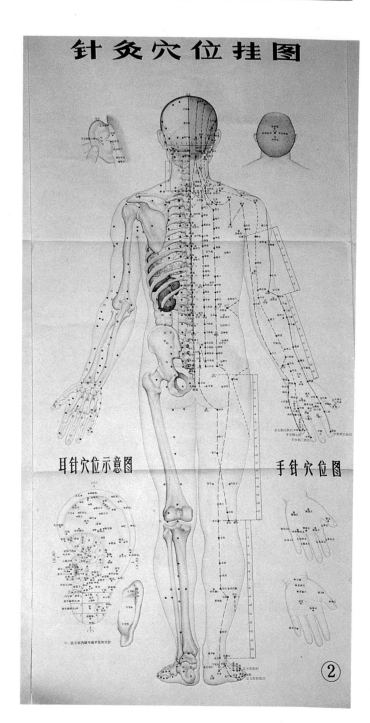

A modern chart of acupuncture points showing both traditional points on the meridians and extra points such as those on the ear and hand.

As a consequence of this growth of serious interest, courses were set up and then schools established for training. Serious schools now offer three-year courses, which include a firm foundation in Western anatomy, physiology and pathology. Clinical training is included, although increasingly it is common to extend this practical study in the hospital facilities of China, where a broader variety of cases can be seen.

In Britain, the Council for Acupuncture was formed in 1982, as an umbrella group uniting the various professional bodies with a common Code of Ethics, Code of Practice and recognized standards of sterilization. (See Chapter 8 for further information.) A similar organization, the American Association of Acupuncture and Oriental Medicine exists in the USA.

Compared to the serious training of traditional acupuncturists – both in Europe and in China itself – the training courses offered to Western doctors, which are really little more than 'familiarization' courses held over several weekends, are ludicrously inadequate. Consequently, most orthodox medical doctors, having never studied acupuncture seriously, are completely ignorant of its depth.

On the other hand, it is to be welcomed that acupuncture is at least given some attention now. The danger, however, is that patients may think they have been treated by (traditional) acupuncture when of course they have not! If such oversimplified treatment fails, because of the inadequacy of the practitioner's training, this may either bring acupuncture into disrepute or lower the standard to an unacceptable and ineffective level.

To have communication between the two systems is of course to be hoped for – but a level of mutual respect and understanding is required. After all, it is not acceptable for acupuncturists to spend a few weekends studying surgery and then call themselves surgeons!

Future directions

It is to be hoped that the future will see the full development of acupuncture in the world, with the establishment of more schools with still higher standards of training. Traditional Chinese medicine offers a comprehensive, integrated and well-tested theory: its application in acupuncture, which is inexpensive, non-invasive, safe and effective, is surely a key form of treatment for the future.

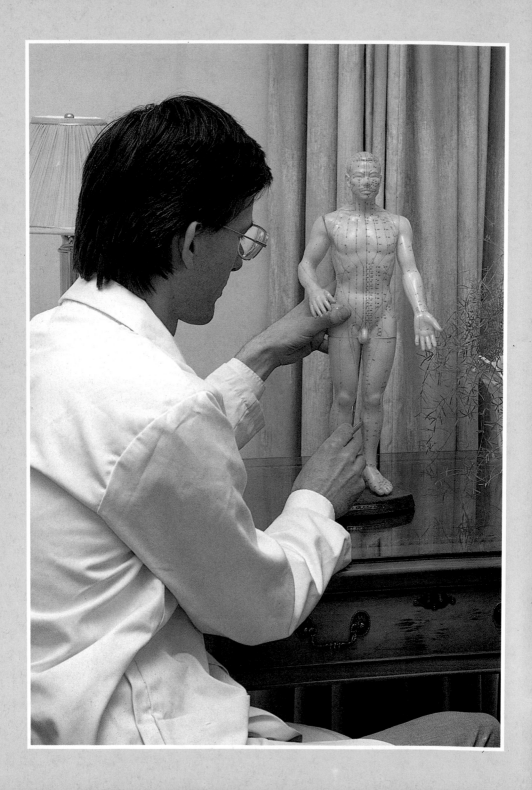

8

FINDING
AND CONSULTING
AN ACUPUNCTURIST

A modern Chinese figure showing the acupuncture meridians is used to explain the treatment to the patient.

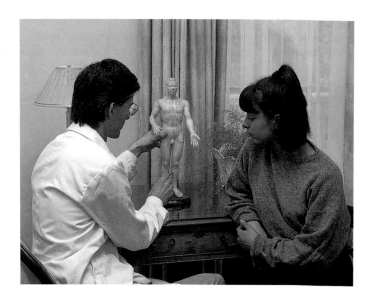

ferrals tend to be dominated by patients who have been given all the drug or surgical treatment possible within the orthodox medical system without this achieving significant success. As a last resort they are referred to acupuncture. Of course, this makes the acupuncturist's task very difficult, and underlines emphatically the advice that, if you feel you may benefit from alternative treatment, try it sooner rather than later.

Acupuncturists see many of the casualties of Western orthodox medicine because of this 'last resort' attitude. Consequently, they look forward to the time when they will see more patients at a time when treatment can be most beneficial, and thereby prevent the unnecessary and often damaging use of costly drug therapy or surgery.

If you benefit from acupuncture treatment it is always a good idea to tell your family doctor, because this can be a great help in promoting understanding between the two professions.

Medication
Always tell your acupuncturist if you are taking medication, even if you feel that it is in no way connected with the problem at hand. Different drugs affect the body in different ways, and it is important for the acupuncturist to take the effect of medication into consideration in a diagnosis.

Your acupuncturist may suggest that you cut down on certain forms of medication, and this is the main area in which cooperation with the prescribing doctor is most useful. Registered acupuncturists all have a basic knowledge of pharmacology and will not suggest any action that would be harmful to the patient.

Steroid drugs, in particular, must be treated with great care, because sudden drops in dosage may produce unpleasant side-effects. If you wish to stop taking or to reduce any medication, your doctor will advise you about the safest procedure. In certain cases, for example insulin-dependent diabetics, patients are able to monitor their own condition, and change dosage levels as required, but should never vary from the recommended regime without prior consultation with the prescribing doctor.

Acupuncture can be helpful in the treatment of anxiety, depression and insomnia, and has also helped in a great many cases of dependence on the drugs prescribed to alleviate these conditions.

Sterilization

All registered acupuncturists are required by law to sterilize needles. It is, of course, in their own interest as much as the patients, to use extreme caution. Public concern about the AIDS virus has led some practitioners to use disposable needles, but these are necessarily of inferior quality and some acupuncturists would prefer to work with better quality needles. Sterilization procedures are more than adequate to deal with the AIDS virus; they were in fact created to eliminate the Hepatitis B virus, which is much more resilient.

In Japan, where many practitioners use gold and silver needles, the acupuncturist will often keep a set of needles in a sterile container for each patient, thus ensuring that one person's needles are never used for another.

Before undergoing any acupuncture treatment it is essential to ask the practitioner about his or her sterilization procedures. Some practitioners will have a sterilizer (called an autoclave) in the clinic, others may use hospital sterilization services. Many practitioners will use disposable needles if the patient is unduly worried, and though the standards of sterilization set by the government have been satisfactorily proven, disposable needles do provide foolproof security. Do not be afraid to ask for them, if you prefer.

9

USEFUL
INFORMATION

USEFUL ADDRESSES

National Associations and Registers

United Kingdom

The Council for Acupuncture
179 Gloucester Place, London NW1 6DX

British Acupuncture Association and Register
34 Alderney Street, London SW1V 4EU

International Register of Oriental Medicine
4 The Manor House, Colley Lane, Reigate,
Surrey RH2 9JW

Register of Traditional Chinese Medicine
19 Trinity Road, London N2 8JJ

Traditional Acupuncture Society
1 The Ridgeway, Stratford-upon-Avon,
Warwickshire CV37 9JL

The United States

National Council of Colleges of Acupuncture and Oriental
Medicine (NCCAOM)
National Accreditation Commission for Schools and
Colleges of Acupuncture and Oriental Medicine (NAC-
SCAOM)
National Commission for the Certification of
Acupuncturists (NCCA)
1424 16th Street NW, Suite 501
Washington, DC 20036

American Association of Acupuncture and Oriental
Medicine (AAAOM)
4101 Lake Boone Trail, Suite 201
Raleigh, NC 27607

Australia

Acupuncture Association of Victoria
126 Union Road, Surrey Hills,
Victoria 3127, Australia

Australian Acupuncture Ethics and Standards
Organization
PO Box 84, Merrylands,
New South Wlales 2160, Australia

Acupuncture Colleges

United Kingdom

The British College of Acupuncture
8 Hunter Street, London WC1N 1BN
(Offers a part-time course for students with basic medical
qualifications)

The International College of Oriental Medicine (UK)
Green Hedges House, Green Hedges Avenue,
East Grinstead, Sussex RH19 1DZ
(Offers a three-year full-time course)

London School of Acupuncture and Traditional Chinese
Medicine
36 Featherstone Street, London EC1Y 8QX
(Weekend courses over three years)

The College of Traditional Chinese Acupuncture (UK),
Tao House, Queensway, Leamington Spa,
Warwickshire CV31 3LZ
(Weekend courses over three years)

The London Academy of Oriental Medicine
129 Queen's Crescent, London NW5 4HE

Northern College of Acupuncture
124 Acomb Road, York YO2 4EY

The College of Integrated Chinese Medicine
40 College Road, Reading RG6 1QB

The United States

Note: These are only a sample of U.S. schools; for a complete list write to NCCAOM (address in previous section).

Emperor's College of Traditional Oriental Medicine
1807B Wilshire Boulevard
Santa Monica, CA 90403

New England School of Acupuncture
30 Common Street
Watertown, MA 02712

Oregon College of Oriental Medicine
10525 SE Cherry Blossom Drive
Portland, OR 97216

Samra University of Oriental Medicine
2828 Beverly Boulevard
Los Angeles, CA 90057

Southwest Acupuncture College
712 West San Mateo
Santa Fe, NM 87501

FURTHER READING

Acupuncture

Robert O Becker and Gary Selden
The Body Electric: Electromagnetism and the Foundations of Life
William Morrow, New York 1985

Fritjof Capra
The Tao of Physics
Fontana, London 1978; Bantam, New York 1978

Leon Chaitow
The Acupuncture Treatment of Pain
Thorsons, Wellingborough/New York 1983

Dianne M Connelly
Traditional Acupuncture: The Law of the Five Elements
Centre for Traditional Acupuncture, Columbia, Maryland 1975

David Eisenberg
Encounters with Qi: Exploring Chinese Medicine
Norton, New York 1985

Ted Kaptchuk
The Web that has no Weaver
Rider, London 1983

Ted Kaptchuk and Michael Crowther
The Healing Arts
BBC Publications, London 1986

Lao Tsu (translated by Gia-Fu Feng and Jane English)
Tao te Ching
Wildwood House, London 1973

Claude Larre, Jean Schatz and Elisabeth Rochat de la Vallée
Survey of Traditional Chinese Medicine
The Ricci Institute, Paris
Traditional Acupuncture Foundation, Columbia, Maryland 1986

Ruth Lever
Acupuncture for Everyone
Penguin, London 1987

Lu Gwei-Djen and Joseph Needham
Celestial Lancets: A History and Rationale of Acupunture and Moxa
Cambridge University Press 1980

Yoshio Manake and Ian A Urquhart
The Layman's Guide to Acupuncture
John Weatherill, New York 1972

Felix Mann
Acupuncture: The Ancient Chinese Art of Acupuncture and How it works scientifically
Vintage Books, New York 1983

Acupuncture: How it Works and How it is used Today
Heinemann/Pan, London 1971, 1985

Matsumoto and Birch
Five Element and Ien Stems
Paradigm Publications, Brookline, Massachussetts 1983

Michael Nightingale
Acupuncture
Optima, London 1987

Joseph Needham
The Great Titration: Science and Society in East and West
George Allen and Unwin, Toronto 1969

Manfred Porkert
Theoretical Foundations of Chinese Medicine
MIT Press, Cambridge Massachusetts 1974

Ilza Veith (translator)
The Yellow Emperor's Classic of Internal Medicine
(a partial translation of the *Nei Jing*)
University of California Press, Berkeley and London 1972

FURTHER READING

General

Boston Women's Health Collective
(Angela Phillips and Jill Rakusen eds)
Our Bodies, Our Selves
Penguin/Boston Women's Collective 1978

Fritjof Capra
The Turning Point
Fontana, London 1983; Simon & Schuster, New
    York 1982

Sheila Ernst and Lucy Goodison
In Our Own Hands: A Book of Self-Help Therapy
Women's Press, London 1981

Dr S J Fulder
A Handbook of Complementary Medicine
Coronet Books, London 1984

Ann Hill (ed)
A Visual Encylopedia of Unconventional Medicine
New English Library, London 1979

Hong-yen Hsu
How to Treat Yourself with Chinese Herbs
Keats Publishing, New Canaan, Connecticut 1993

Hong-yen Hsu and Douglas Peacher (eds)
Shang Han Lun: Wellspring of Chinese Medicine
Keats Publishing, New Canaan, Connecticut 1994

Ivan Illich
Limits to Medicine: Medical Nemesis
Calder & Boyars, London 1976; Penguin 1977

Brian Inglis
The Diseases of Civilization
Hodder & Stoughton, London 1981

Natural Medicine
Collins, London 1980

Brain Inglis and Ruth West
The Alternative Health Guide
Michael Joseph/Mermaid, London 1983

Leslie J Kaslof (ed)
Wholistic Dimensions in Healing: A Resource Guide
Doubleday, New York 1978

Gerald Kogan (ed)
*Your Body Works: A Guide to Health, Energy and
    Balance*
Transform, Berkeley, California 1980

E K Ledermann
Good Health through Natural Therapy
Kogan Page, London 1976

Daniel B. Mowrey
Herbal Tonic Therapies
Keats Publishing, New Canaan, Connecticut 1993

Patrick C Pietroni
Holistic Medicine: Old Map, New Territory
British Journal of Holistic Medicine, vol 1, London
    1984

Chris Thompson and Denis Maceoin
The Health Crisis
The Natural Medicines Society, Birmingham 1987

Richard Totman
Social Causes of Illness
Souvenir Press, London 1979

Michael van Straten
The Natural Health Consultant
Ebury Press, London 1987

Dr A Vogel
The Nature Doctor
Keats Publishing, New Canaan, Connecticut 1992

INDEX

INDEX

INDEX

ACKNOWLEDGMENTS

With thanks for assistance provided by Robert Duggan, President, the Traditional Acupuncture Institute, Maryland.

The publishers would also like to thank the following organizations and individuals for their kind permission to reproduce the illustrations in this book:

Ancient Art & Architecture Collection: 37, 53, 83, 121, 134 above, 137 **Aspect Picture Library:** 52 **The Bridgeman Art Library/Mauritshuis, The Hague:** 47 **Stephanie Colasanti:** 80 above **E T Archive/National Palace Museum, Taiwan:** 55, 132, 135/**British Museum:** 60 **Mary Evans Picture Library:** 46 **Sally & Richard Greenhill:** 118, 126, 129, 130 **Robert Harding Picture Library:** 131, 142, 150 **Michael Holford:** 68 **The Hutchison Library:** 43 **Octopus Publishing Group:** J. Sims 80 below/J. Harpur 88/A. Hornak 119, 123 above, 123 below **Popperfoto:** 49 **Ann Ronan Picture Library:** 48 **Science Photo Library:** 33,36/ **Malcolm Fielding, The BOC Group PLC:** 38 **Tony Stone Photo Library:** 56, 87 **John Watney:** 10, 133 **The Wellcome Institute Library, London:** 2, 7, 134 below **Zefa:** 19, 23, 24, 139

The following photographs were specially taken by Peter Chadwick: 6, 12, 13, 28, 31, 74, 92, 93, 95, 96, 98, 99, 101, 103, 104, 105, 106 above, 106 below, 107, 108, 110, 125, 144, 145, 148, 151, 152, 153

We would also like to thank the author, the **Hale Clinic, London,** and practitioners, and Acumedic Centre Ltd for their help with these photographs.

Illustrations by Elaine Anderson

Editor Viv Croot   **Art Editor** Alyson Kyles
Coordinating Editor Camilla Simmons   **Designer** Malcolm Smythe

Production Alyssum Ross

Picture research Angie Grant, Christina Weir